WOMEN AND WORK IN
DEVELOPING SOCIETIES

Women and Work in Developing Societies

NADIA HAGGAG YOUSSEF

GREENWOOD PRESS, PUBLISHERS
WESTPORT, CONNECTICUT

Library of Congress Cataloging in Publication Data

Youssef, Nadia Haggag.
  Women and work in developing societies.

    Reprint of the ed. published by the Institute of
International Studies, University of California,
Berkeley, which was issued as no. 15 of the Popula-
tion monograph series.
    Bibliography: p. 129-137.
    Includes index.
    1. Underdeveloped areas--Women's employment.
I. Title. II. Series: Population monograph se-
ries ; no. 15.
[HD6223.Y55 1976]   331.4'09172'4   76-4537
ISBN 0-8371-8836-9

Originally published in 1974 by University of California, Berkeley

Reprinted with the permission of The Regents of the University
of California, acting on behalf of its International Population
and Urban Research

Reprinted in 1976 by Greenwood Press,
a division of Williamhouse-Regency Inc.

Library of Congress Catalog Card Number 76-4537

ISBN 0-8371-8836-9

Printed in the United States of America

Foreword to the Greenwood Press Edition

The high birth rates of less developed countries can fall to replacement level only if the women of those countries acquire alternatives to home and motherhood. The most likely alternative is that of outside employment, which not only takes women's time but gives them contacts with a wider world and the independence and satisfaction of earning an economic reward as individuals, apart from the family.

But how is this alternative to be realized? As is well known, the less developed countries are caught in a vicious circle. Population growth is rapid because of low death rates and high birth rates. Yet employing women outside the home, which might lower the birth rate, is discouraged by widespread unemployment, itself a result of rapid population growth. This discouragement reinforces the traditional institutions restricting female to the home; thus high fertility is perpetuated.

If all less developed countries were alike, the outlook might seem hopeless, but fortunately this is not the case. In Latin American countries, for example, women enter outside employment more frequently than they do in Muslim countries. If we can understand that difference, perhaps we can get at the key factors governing female labor-force participation in developing countries and thus determine what policies would raise that participation.

It is exactly that task that Professor Youssef sets for herself in the present study, and it is a task to which she is ideally suited. Being Egyptian, she is thoroughly acquainted with Muslim institutions; yet, having lived in Mexico, she also is familiar with Latin American society.

A simple-minded answer to the question might be that "attitudes" differ in the two types of society. This is true, but the important question is why they differ. Dr. Youssef probes deeper to find differences in social structure, in rewards and penalties. She penetrates to the mechanisms of social control and seeks to learn how certain aspects of modernization tend to affect these mechanisms. Hers is, therefore, a sociological and demographic analysis, not a description of presumed attitudes.

Her analysis complements others done at IPUR. This series, Studies in Population and Urban Demography, includes books on one or another aspect of Latin American demography and a volume by Valerie Oppenheimer on The Female Labor Force in the United States, but the present volume is the only one to make an in-depth comparison between Muslim and Latin American societies on a demographically significant subject.

It is a pleasure to acknowledge Dr. Youssef's unique contribution to our list of studies.

Kingsley Davis

International Population and Urban Research
Institute of International Studies
University of California, Berkeley
January 25, 1976

FOREWORD

In analyzing a particular society a social scientist enjoys an advantage if he knows the society intimately from having lived in it, for he can then sense the motives and feelings of the members. When different societies are being compared, this advantage is normally lacking: no one can grow up in several societies at once. There are, however, investigators who happen to have lived in at least two distinct societies. The author of the present volume is one of these. Professor Youssef lived most of her life in Egypt, but she also spent part of her girlhood in Mexico. She is therefore in a favorable position to compare Muslim with Latin American societies not only in statistical terms (which anyone can do) but also in institutional and motivational terms. This is fortunate, because the subject of her comparative analysis--the labor-force participation of women--is delicate.

The degree to which the women of a country enter the labor force outside the home is associated not only with the country's level of income but with other conditions as well. Certain Muslim countries rival certain Latin American countries in development, yet their female labor force is smaller. Why? A simple-minded answer is that "attitudes" differ in the two types of society. Quite so, but again why? Dr. Youssef probes deeper to find differences in social structure, in rewards and penalties. She is interested in the mechanisms of social control and in how development alters these mechanisms. The attitudes about the role that women *should* have tend to shift long after the role itself has changed.

Dr. Youssef's study complements other studies also done at IPUR. The Population Monograph Series includes previous volumes on one or another aspect of Latin American demography and one volume on the female labor force. Hers, however, is the only one to make an in-depth comparison between Muslim and Latin American societies in regard to a demographically significant subject. It is a pleasure to welcome her unique contribution to our list of studies.

Kingsley Davis

International Population and Urban Research
Berkeley, California

v

ACKNOWLEDGMENTS

This study owes more than can be acknowledged in words to Professor Kingsley Davis whose valuable guidance, stimulating criticism, and unfailing sense of humor have been decisive factors in the final shape in which it now stands. To him my deepest gratitude.

Thanks are also due to Dr. Samuel Preston who devoted valuable time in pointing out fruitful directions in the labor-force analysis, and to Professor Robert Bellah for his expert suggestions on the history of Islam in the Middle East and of Catholicism in Latin America.

The help of all members of the International Population and Urban Research Center at Berkeley is gratefully acknowledged, in particular that of Dr. Eduardo Arriaga for initiating the writer in the by-ways of quantitative techniques and encouraging her throughout the difficult phases.

The initial data for this research were collected under a research-apprenticeship grant from the Institute of International Studies, University of California, Berkeley, to whom the writer expresses her thanks.

CONTENTS

LIST OF TABLES

Chapter 1

INTRODUCTION

Despite the considerable literature on the subject of economic development, very little systematic comparative work has focused on female labor force participation in developing countries. Generally, the literature emphasizes capital investment because lack of labor supply has never been envisaged as a crucial issue, the assumption being that the major problem is, conversely, an over-abundance of untrained male labor. Women, who are considered as only secondarily involved in potential labor force participation, have been largely ignored. In recent years, however, professional demographers and economic development planners have become increasingly aware that women's gainful employment outside the home is relevant to policies aimed at reducing rates of population growth in the developing world.

As far as the currently developing nations are concerned, two basic problems require urgent confrontation. First, high fertility is proving to be a major obstacle in raising per capita income. No matter how ambitious and successful projects designed to promote economic growth may be, sheer population pressure rapidly reaches a point where the standard of living is driven down faster than economic development can lift it. Second, education in the advisability of birth control methods does not in itself guarantee widespread application, nor does it ensure female endorsement of family limitation. Women will continue desiring and bearing more children for as long as family-building activities are socially rewarding [Davis, 1967].

From the standpoint of population policy, current demographic interest in the subject of female labor force participation in developing countries stems from the realization that the employment of women is one of the more effective structural means by which nonfamilial roles begin to offer significant competition to familial ones as avenues for reward and satisfactions, thereby influencing fertility in general and family-size motivation in particular [Blake, 1965:1195]. In high fertility societies, where female status in the social structure depends almost exclusively upon the ability to produce at least a minimum number of children, women are impelled to seek the idealized role of wife and mother. Work participation has been documented to be a fertility-level depressant and, when properly rewarded, to

1

offer women an alternative career which makes delayed marriage and smaller families attractive.[1]

Given the possibility that the economic utilization of women could have a negative effect on fertility and consequently contribute to the rise of per capita income in developing countries, the consequent desire to accelerate female labor force participation by according it high priority in development strategy is understandable [Collver and Langlois, 1962:367]. However, to be able to count on accelerated participation one must first consider systematically the structural factors that influence women to join the labor force.

Why women become involved in work activities is the issue at the core of this study. Latin America and the Middle East, similar in their stages of industrialization and economic development, widely different in their social and cultural systems, provide a unique opportunity to examine the interrelationships among women workers, social structure, and economic development.

Sociological Perspectives on Female Labor Force Participation

The sociological interpretation of women's participation in the nonagricultural work force has been bipolarized. One view tends to categorize female employment rates as a function of the level of economic development [Wilensky, 1968:238]--a position clearly supported by the experience of the now-industrialized world. Hence, female involvement in economic activities outside of agriculture will occur as an end product of increased educational and occupational opportunities accompanying industrialization. Insofar as developing countries are concerned, economic changes similar to those triggered by the industrial revolution in the West must occur before a large-scale involvement of women in the work force can be expected.

The other view emphasizes the premise that the development of the female nonagricultural work force is contingent upon variables related to social organization, particularly upon the prevailing family system [Collver and Langlois, 1962:371]. It is thus assumed that family organization has powerful sources of resistance and is not merely acted upon by accelerated rates of economic development. In underlining the importance of the

---

[1]Relative data for married women during the 1930s and 1940s have been summarized by the United Nations [1953]. Also refer to Collver and Langlois [1962:381], Freedman, Baumart, and Bolte [1959/60]; Axelrod, Freedman, *et al.* [1963]; Freedman, Whelpton, and Campbell [1959]; Jaffe [1959:chap. 10]; Pratt and Whelpton [1956]; and Ridley [1959].

INTRODUCTION

family system as a patterning force of female employment, this view considers that a woman's first responsibility is to her home and her immediate family: "her key roles have been and remain those of the wife, mother and homemaker; and even when she is not married, her expectations of assuming these roles exercise an influence on the character and extent of her economic activities" [Collver and Langlois, 1962:371].

The course which women eventually take with respect to work will depend on the extent to which they are able to make "adjustments" between their family and their economic roles. Collver and Langois, taking into account the historic relationship between the organization of the economy and the prevailing family system, suggest that these adjustments may follow one of four basic patterns:

--*The industrial society pattern:* women's participation is high. High wages and the desire for better living standards oppose the persisting notions of woman's belonging in the home and being spared from paid productive labor. This counterplay puts an upper limit on participation rates. Women postpone marriage temporarily or work after marriage until children are born, and frequently return to the labor force later.

--*The Latin American pattern:* women's nondomestic participation is low. Young girls, often immigrants from rural areas, are given an interval for wage work as domestics. Temporary postponement of marriage is permitted for some sectors of society.

--*The Caribbean pattern:* women's participation rate is high. The family system is weak and unstable; illegitimacy rates are high; many women need to be self-sufficient at numerous intervals throughout their lives.

--*The Muslim Middle East pattern:* women's participation rate is very low. Women marry early, attend exclusively to husband and children, and are secluded through prohibitions on public activity.

In the experience of the North European countries, industrialization brought about far-reaching changes in women's participation in economic activities outside of agriculture. Correlative with the economic and occupational opportunities provided by the new economy, there was an influx of women into gainful employment as a result of complex factors related to female emancipation and to changes of sex roles in the traditional division of labor within marriage. The transition from a subsistence economy to the industrialized market levels caused a change in the structure and particularly in the functions of the family. This occurred in the wake of moving the center of production from the household to the factory, and later through industry

3

supplanting the home as the source of an increasing number of
services and goods. Corresponding with these changes were increased opportunities for women's education, their right to participate in political life, and their partial relief from the
burden of childbearing. All combined, these innovations were
sufficiently fundamental to effect changes in the character and
organization of the Western family and as a consequence to restructure the role of the Western woman in relation to society
[Jaffe and Stewart, 1951:350-353; Klein, 1963/64:25].

To what extent were these changes due to the needs of the
industrial system? To what extent were they due to the institutional arrangements peculiar to Western society? It becomes
extremely difficult to isolate one cause from the other, particularly since theories in sociology and economic development have
leaned heavily on the background of Western Europe and the English-
speaking countries of the New World. We can ask ourselves, however, whether the experience of the now-industrialized Western
world is being repeated by countries currently in the process of
industrialization. An examination of the experience of Latin
American and Middle Eastern countries will hopefully clarify
many of the assumptions that have been made on the basis of the
Western model regarding the impact of industrialization upon
family organization, in general, and the status of women, in
particular.

This comparative study of Latin America and the Middle
East derives broader significance from the fact that the countries
of these two regions are characterized, generally, by a similar
level of economic development. They have in common a lack of
industrialization, an economic dependence on the industrialized
world, a rapid population increase, and a considerable degree of
urbanization. Despite these similarities the two regions are
characterized by pronounced differences in the participation rates
of women in nonagricultural economic activities. Whereas virtually all countries in Latin America exhibit high female nonagricultural employment rates (averaging nearly 20 percent), the
Middle Eastern countries systematically report the lowest female
activity rates on record (less than 4 percent). Among every
100 workers engaged in nonagricultural activities, more than
one-third are female in Latin America, only *one-eleventh* in the
Middle East!

To be able to gauge more closely aspects of the inter-
relationship between economic development and women's involvement in the nonagricultural work force, this study embarks on an
intensive and systematic analysis of thirteen countries within
the Latin American and Middle Eastern regions. The purpose is
to identify some of the critical independent variables that influence the extent to which women participate in employment outside of agricultural work.

4

These countries are: Chile, Colombia, Costa Rica, Ecuador, Mexico, and Peru in Latin America; Egypt, Iran, Libya, Morocco, Pakistan, Syria, and Turkey in the Middle East.

Organization of the Study

The departure point is an examination of the contemporary relationship between economic development and women's participation in the nonagricultural labor force in industrialized and nonindustrialized countries. By charting historical changes during the nascent period of industrialization in the United States, and by comparing the findings with the degree of economic development associated with women's involvement in the nonagricultural economic sector in currently developing countries, the concept of a consistently positive relationship between economic development levels and female participation in the nonagricultural work force will be put to the test. The question--Are currently developing countries in actuality repeating the pattern of the now-industrialized West?--is answered with a compelling negative. In all Middle Eastern societies women are not responding to higher levels of economic development with a parallel increase in their work participation rates in nonagricultural activities. In the Latin American countries high rates of female activity are sustained independent of economic development levels. The evidence is sufficient that women's work involvement does not operate in accordance with the axioms of economic theories.

The remainder of our study offers a systematic exploration of this problem in an attempt to account for the contrasting experience of women workers in the thirteen countries selected to represent the Latin American and Middle Eastern regions.

Chapter III inquires into whether or not the differentials in female employment rates can be explained by regional differences in the structure of demand for workers in the labor market. A detailed comparison of the industrial composition and the occupational distribution of the total nonagricultural labor force is undertaken to identify possible sources of differences with respect to the occupational opportunities that are available to women in the labor market of each region.

Chapters IV and V address the task of identifying influential conditions which control the supply of women available to the labor market, independently of demand. Chapter IV deals with comparative differences in female educational standards between the Latin American and Middle Eastern countries and tests the impact such differences bear upon women's actual propensity to seek and obtain employment.

In Chapter V the substance of population differences with
respect to family characteristics centrally related to woman's
employability is investigated. Specifically, the investigation
is directed toward examining the marital and fertility characteristics of the female population in Latin America and the Middle
East for the purpose of testing through standardization procedures
whether or not these demographic characteristics have a positive
bearing upon the female employment rates.

In the final analysis of differences, Chapter VI embarks
upon the crucial issue of who controls the decision that women may
or may not work in Latin American and Middle Eastern societies
This chapter deals with regional variations in the structure of
social control, their sources, and their consequences by singling
out significant analogies and equally significant differences
between the machinery of social control in both types of societies.

In Chapter VII the relevance of systems of social control
as major determinants of the extent to which women participate in
the nonagricultural labor force is emphasized by examining the
impact of differences in the structure of control upon the institutional position of the woman in Latin American and Middle
Eastern societies. The position of the married and the nonmarried woman in the social structure is examined separately,
with particular emphasis upon the social context in which participation in the work force takes place.

The Data Available

The latest available data were used from the official
census populations of the thirteen countries selected for intensive analysis. The data presented also draw on the United
Nations Demographic Yearbooks, on the International Labor Office
Yearbooks, and the UNESCO Statistical Yearbooks.

Students of developing countries are only too well aware
of the problems involved in any such enterprise. Reported
shrinkages or substantial increases in the labor force are often
due to changing definitions and methods used in identifying the
economically active segment of the population. In industrialized
countries the distinction between economic and noneconomic activity is clear cut. In developing countries, by contrast, the distinction between household chores and economic activity is still
somewhat artificial, and the differentiation depends to a large
extent on subjective judgments of the officials involved.

This difficulty has been partly circumvented in our
study. First, by focusing exclusively on the nonagricultural
labor force, the bulk of marginal workers who fall under the
category of "unpaid" family workers have been excluded. Second,

6

in order to achieve a common denominator, most of the computations include only women workers aged fifteen and older. In this way it has been possible to avoid not only the differential in employment rates resulting from the inclusion of young girls, who in certain developing countries constitute an important portion of the female labor force, but also to ensure that many of the "unpaid" female workers are excluded.

Many more aspects of the female nonagricultural labor force could have been investigated in this research if national and international agencies responsible for the compilation of data had made a distinction between the agricultural and the nonagricultural categories. A considerable number of the tabulations cross-classifying data had to be rejected because of the impossibility of separating the nonagricultural sector from the total productive population.

Census returns undoubtedly contain errors as a result of either the under- or the over-enumeration of women in the labor force. The statistics used in this work are not less precise than those typical of developing nations as a whole. Most important, the uses to which the data have been put, as well as the conclusions drawn, have required relative accuracy rather than perfection. Had other studies of nonagricultural women workers in Latin America and the Middle East been available, they would have served to assist not only in the evaluation of the census material but also in supplementing the data in their more critical aspects. This shortcoming has been only partially rectified by the author's first-hand knowledge of the two regions under consideration through a lengthy residence in Mexico and as a native of Egypt.

Chapter 2

FEMALE PARTICIPATION IN NONAGRICULTURAL ACTIVITIES
AND LEVEL OF ECONOMIC DEVELOPMENT

An overall scanning of international data emphasizes
the striking diversity and variation of female participation in
the labor force. Certain countries report many of their womenfolk as economically active; others report only a slight proportion. Much of this variability is due to problems of compara-
bility of data, particularly with respect to agricultural work,
and to contradictory definitions and methods used in identifying
the economically active segment of the population. But even when
one considers female participation in the nonagricultural economic
sector, which is a better defined and restricted segment and where
labor force concepts have a more precise meaning and measurement,
there are still pronounced differences in the female employment
rates between one country and another. Switzerland and Jamaica,
for instance, report 35 percent of all adult women as active
labor force members; in Ecuador the corresponding proportion is
22 percent, whereas in Pakistan and in Turkey only two adult
women in every 100 are working outside the agricultural sector.

What can account for these differentials between countries?
What factors influence or determine the extent to which women participate in the labor force, and the particular pattern this participation takes?

Generally, there are at least four types of influence
on female employment in nonagricultural work. From the demand
side: (1) the level of economic development and (2) the specific
organization of the economy. From the supply side: (3) the
level of educational achievement and (4) the marital and fertility
characteristics of the female population.

In this chapter the influence of the level of economic
development upon women's work participation rates in nonagricultural activities is singled out for discussion. The purpose is
to examine its relative importance in explaining differentials
between countries in nonagricultural female employment rates.
The remaining categories are investigated in subsequent chapters.

8

An additional focal point of this chapter is the historical evolution of the female nonagricultural labor force in the
West. The purpose is to compare the experience of the nonindustrialized world with that of the currently developing countries.
Western societies have witnessed far-reaching changes during
their industrial growth with respect to the distribution and
composition of the female labor force, the character of women's
involvement in economic activities, and the female contribution
to economic life. To what extent are those trends being experienced by countries currently in the process of industrialization? By charting historical changes in the evolution of the
female labor force in the United States and by relating those
changes to the contemporary relationship between economic development and female employment rates in the developing countries,
it will be possible to determine if the Western experience as
exemplified by the United States has universal applicability. In
other words, are the currently developing nations repeating the
historical experience of the now-industrialized West?

Female Participation in Nonagricultural Activities

It has become commonplace to cite the level of economic
development as a major determinant in the extent to which women
participate in economic activities outside of agriculture and in
the particular pattern this participation takes. International
comparisons by Collver and Langlois [1962] and Wilensky [1968]
show that developing countries in general have a lower degree
than industrialized nations of female labor force participation
outside of agriculture. Based mainly on data from metropolitan
areas of thirty-eight countries, the Collver-Langlois findings
show the mean female work participation rate in highly industrialized countries to be 39, eight percentage points above the
rate for the less economically developed group. Wilensky's
classification of thirty-four countries by per capita income,
female participation in nonagricultural work, and feminist
ideology shows that nonagricultural labor force participation
of women in the most-developed countries varies according to
ideology, but that the most-industrialized nations have the
highest female participation rates.

That developing countries, in general, have an average
lower female participation in nonagricultural pursuits than
industrialized nations is also shown by a cross-tabulation of
recent data. Table 1 portrays a group of fifty countries
classified into industrialized and underdeveloped according to
per capita income and activity rate of adult males in nonagricultural work. The importance of the female component is
measured in terms of women's work participation rate in the
nonagricultural sector. It is clear that women score a higher
average participation in the advanced economies. The mean female

9

TABLE 1

CONTEMPORARY ASSOCIATION BETWEEN ECONOMIC DEVELOPMENT AND FEMALE
PARTICIPATION IN NONAGRICULTURAL ECONOMIC ACTIVITIES (c. 1960)

Industrial- ized Countries (inc./capita =U.S. $500+)	Activity Rate		Population (millions)		Under- developed Countries (inc./capita < U.S. $500)	Activity Rate		Population (millions)	
	Male	Fe- male	Male	Fe- male		Male	Fe- male	Male	Fe- male
Total	64.3	28.1	216.4	232.9	Total	35.1	12.3	274.3	267.9
United Kingdom	78.6	40.4	19.5	21.6	*Class I*				
					Chile	56.1	21.8	2.1	2.3
Germany	78.4	35.1	19.4	22.7	Portugal	48.2	14.0	2.9	3.4
Switzerland	74.9	34.3	2.0	2.1	Puerto Rico[b]	46.2	19.7	0.7	0.7
Australia	74.3	27.8	3.7	3.6	Iraq	44.6	2.6	1.7	1.8
Netherlands[a]	72.5	21.9	3.9	4.0	Greece	41.9	12.2	2.9	3.2
					Costa Rica	40.9	16.3	0.3	0.4
					Jamaica[b]	40.5	35.7	0.5	0.5
United States[b]	71.5	32.0	61.3	65.0	Egypt	40.1	3.5	7.3	7.5
					Rumania[b]	40.0	12.6	6.2	6.8
Canada	66.5	28.4	6.1	6.0	*Class II*				
Luxembourg	65.6	22.2	0.1	0.1	Iran	39.6	7.0	5.6	5.4
Denmark[a]	65.5	35.9	1.7	1.8	Peru	39.5	15.3	2.8	2.9
Austria	64.9	31.2	2.5	3.1	Panama	38.6	23.3	0.3	0.3
					Morocco	38.4	4.5	3.2	3.3
Sweden[a]	64.6	31.4	2.9	3.0	Turkey	36.4	2.7	8.2	8.1
Argentina[b]	64.3	22.4	7.1	7.1	Syria	35.0	3.2	1.2	1.2
France	62.8	29.3	16.7	18.2	Ecuador	34.9	21.8	1.2	1.3
Norway	62.7	22.9	1.3	1.3	Tunisia	34.9	4.4	1.1	0.9
Japan	62.6	28.8	31.5	33.8	India	31.9	8.8	133.6	125.2
					Mexico[a]	30.6	12.0	12.5	13.0
Venezuela[a]	61.7	20.0	1.8	1.7	*Class III*				
Israel[b]	58.4	22.0	0.7	0.7	Nicaragua	29.4	19.0	0.4	0.4
Italy[b]	57.3	24.2	18.9	20.1	Korea[a]	29.1	9.1	7.3	8.1
Hungary	56.4	25.7	3.5	3.9	El Salvador	28.1	17.4	0.7	0.7
Finland	52.5	33.0	1.5	1.6	Indonesia	26.9	10.9	27.0	28.7
					Pakistan	26.4	2.3	26.6	23.5
Poland	50.8	24.1	9.3	10.5	Philippines	26.1	18.2	7.2	7.3
Ireland[b]	48.6	24.0	1.0	1.0	Honduras	23.9	13.1	0.5	0.5
					Thailand	20.6	11.8	7.4	7.5
					Sudan	14.6	1.6	2.9	3.0

[a]Population <20 for Netherlands and Sweden; 18+ for Denmark;
20+ for Venezuela; 12+ for Mexico; 13+ for Korea.

[b]Population 14 and older.

Sources: Per capita income [Davis, 1972]; population [UN, 1965:
Table 8]; nonagricultural economic workers [UN, 1965:
Table 8], except Pakistan and UK [UN, 1968:Table 2A].

activity rate in the industrialized world is 28.1 percent; in the underdeveloped nations it is 12.3 percent.

Throughout the following discussion the underdeveloped countries are grouped into four levels according to their degree of urbanization:

Class I   - *Highly urbanized countries:* with 25 percent or more of their population in cities of 100,000 or larger.

Class II   - *Semi-urban countries:* with 20 to 25 percent population in cities of 100,000 or larger.

Class III - *Partially urban:* with 15 to 20 percent population in cities of 100,000 or larger.

Class IV   - *Least urban:* with less than 15 percent of the population in cities of 100,000 or larger.

Do Currently Developing Countries Compare with the Historical Experience of the West?

While the cross-sectional comparison in Table 1 establishes the contemporary association between degree of economic development and female participation in nonagricultural work, this comparison does not indicate how currently developing countries relate to the historical experience of the now-industrialized nations. Are underdeveloped countries ahead of, in the same position as, or behind where the now-industrialized nations were at a comparable stage of their economic growth? How has the working population varied historically with economic development, and how has the evolution of the female labor force in particular been affected?

The historical changes in the structure of employment in the United States since 1870 are shown in Table 2. In this table the degree of urbanization, as measured by the percentage of population living in cities of 100,000 and larger, is taken as an index of economic development.[1] According to this indicator the close association between economic development and the proportion of women engaged in nonagricultural economic activities is confirmed. The period extending from 1870 to 1930 is particularly suited for comparative purposes because it marks the rising tide of industrialization in the United States. During those six decades the percent population residing in cities of

[1]For discussion of the close association between the process of urbanization and economic development, refer to Davis [1954:6-26].

TABLE 2

HISTORICAL TREND OF FEMALE PARTICIPATION IN
THE NONAGRICULTURAL LABOR FORCE:
UNITED STATES 1870-1960

Date	Urban Population			Nonagricultural Labor Force				
	Total (000s)	In Cities of 100,000+ (000s)	Percent	Number (000s)	Percent of Total	Females (000s)	Female Activity Rate	Female Percent of Total
1870	39,818	4,129	10.6	6,490	47.0	1,466	10.2	14.8
1890	62,947	9,697	15.4	13,750	58.0	3,205	14.0	18.0
1900	75,994	14,208	18.7	18,142	63.0	4,311	15.3	23.8
1910	91,972	20,302	22.1	25,686	69.1	6,270	18.2	24.2
1920	105,710	27,429	25.9	30,816	73.0	7,468	18.5	24.2
1930	122,775	36,325	29.6	38,365	78.0	9,844	20.1	26.0
1950	165,563	71,660	43.2	52,046	88.2	15,844		30.4
1960	198,688	98,966	49.8	66,451	97.7	22,022	32.0	33.1

Sources: Data on female labor force before 1900 [Hooks, 1947]; on labor force from
1870 to 1950 [U.S. Bureau of Census, 1960:74]; on population from 1870 to
1930 [U.S. Bureau of Census, 1960:14]; on population in 1950 and 1960
[Davis, 1969:Tables A, B, C]; on labor force distribution for 1960 [U.S.
Bureau of Census, 1960:Table 1].

100,000 nearly trebled (from 11 to 30) and the proportion of the total economically active population in the nonagricultural sector increased from 47 to 78 percent. The female work participation rate in the nonagricultural labor force, in turn, increased from 10 percent in 1870 to 15 percent in 1900, reaching 20 percent in 1930.

How do these historical changes compare with the current situation in the developing nations? Are underdeveloped countries moving in the direction of bringing their female labor force to the standards set by an advanced economy at a comparable period of its economic growth?

For a group of twenty-two underdeveloped countries, Table 3 shows the current relationship between degree of urbanization and participation of women in nonagricultural activities.

As can be seen from Table 3 the differences between levels of urbanization reached by the underdeveloped countries are quite pronounced. Least urban countries manifest about one-third the degree of urbanization characterizing the highly urban nations and one-half that of the semi- and partially urban groups. This classification thus incorporates the range of variation in urbanization and provides a more precise measure for comparative purposes than the average computed for underdeveloped countries as a group.

The comparison between the currently developing countries and the experience of the now-industrialized nations is made by first matching each set of countries according to the average degree of their urbanization with the United States at the corresponding stage of its history. When for all underdeveloped countries the average percentage of population residing in cities of 100,000 or more is computed, it corresponds to the level of urbanization reached by the United States in 1900. However, when differences in urbanization levels are taken into account, the gap between the United States and the currently developing world is reduced considerably. Class IV countries lag 90 years behind, while Class I countries are only 30 years behind the United States (Table 4).

Our next step is to measure whether the evolution of the nonagricultural female labor force in currently developing countries is more or less advanced than the female labor force in the United States was at comparable periods of its economic modernization. This is done by matching underdeveloped countries with the United States by similarities in urbanization levels and then comparing the employment rates.

Taken as a group, underdeveloped countries are slightly behind the standards set by the United States. For example, in

13

TABLE 3

POPULATION CONCENTRATION IN CONTEMPORARY UNDERDEVELOPED
COUNTRIES RELATED TO FEMALE PARTICIPATION IN
NONAGRICULTURAL LABOR (c. 1960)
(in thousands)

Developmental Level and Country	Urban Population			Nonagricultural Labor Force		
	Total	In Cities 100,000+	Percent in Cities 100,000+	Total	Female	Percent Female
Class I = 25 percent or more population in cities 100,000+						
Chile	7,772	2,452	31.5	2,307	502	21.8
Puerto Rico	2,350	656	28.0	721	142	19.7
Greece	8,327	2,285	27.5	3,205	390	12.2
Syria	4,561	1,203	26.4	1,266	37	3.2
Egypt	26,085	6,823	26.2	7,489	260	3.5
Average			27.9			12.2
Class II = 20-25 percent population in cities 100,000+						
Portugal	8,889	2,081	23.4	3,363	471	14.0
Jamaica	1,629	377	23.1	520	186	35.7
South Korea	24,989	5,707	22.8	8,120	735	9.1
Costa Rica	1,171	257	21.9	353	58	16.3
Iraq	6,831	1,460	21.3	1,775	46	2.6
Average			22.5			15.5
Class III = 15-20 percent population in cities 100,000+						
Morocco	11,640	2,200	18.9	3,311	150	4.5
Mexico	34,923	6,512	18.6	9,933	1,303	12.0
Ecuador	4,352	764	17.6	1,256	190	21.8
Iran	21,500	3,732	17.4	5,394	379	7.0
Rumania	18,403	2,982	16.2	6,753	850	12.6
Tunisia	4,157	648	15.6	927	40	4.4
Peru	11,025	1,649	15.0	2,865	438	15.3
Average			17.0			11.0
Class IV = <15 percent population in cities 100,000+						
Philippines	27,088	3,863	14.3	7,319	1,330	18.2
Nicaragua	1,411	197	14.0	415	78	19.0
Turkey	27,510	3,355	12.2	8,104	265	2.7
Indonesia	93,506	9,082	9.2	28,744	3,133	10.9
Pakistan	92,696	6,643	7.2	23,500	543	2.3
Average			11.4			10.6

Sources: Urban population [Davis, 1969: Tables A, B, C]; nonagricultural economic workers [UN, 1965: Table 8],
except Pakistan [UN, 1968: Table 2a].

TABLE 4

LEVEL OF UNDERDEVELOPED COUNTRIES' URBANIZATION AND
FEMALE NONAGRICULTURAL PARTICIPATION COMPARED
WITH THE UNITED STATES

Class of Country	Year	Percent Population in Cities 100,000+	Percent Female Participation
Average of all underdeveloped countries	1960	19.4	12.3
United States	1900	18.7	15.3
Class I - most urban	1960	27.9	12.2
United States	1930	29.6	20.1
Class II - semi-urban	1960	22.5	15.5
United States	1910	22.1	18.2
Class III - partially urban	1960	17.0	11.0
United States	1900	18.7	15.3
Class IV - least urban	1960	11.4	10.6
United States	1870	10.6	10.0

Sources: See Tables 1, 2, and 3.

the United States in 1900 female employment rates in nonfarm
work were 15.3 percent; in currently developing countries the
corresponding average is 12.3 percent. The situation becomes
more complex when differences in the degree of urbanization
within the developing world are taken into account.

The general findings emerging from this comparison are
that Classes I, II, and III fail to match the evolution of the
female labor force in the United States. Only in the least urbanized countries does the female employment rate approximate
the rates in the United States at a comparable period of its
urbanization history. The discrepancy in rates between the
underdeveloped nations and the historical experience of the
United States is most evident among the Class I countries.
According to their urbanization level these countries approximate
conditions in the United States in 1930, when twenty women per
hundred were gainfully employed. In the most urban underdeveloped
countries the corresponding percentage is only twelve.

Two possible explanations for this trend are: one, the
tendency in certain underdeveloped countries for urbanization to
run ahead of industrial development; and two, the possibility
that in certain societies women do not respond to higher levels
of economic development with a parallel increase in their work-
participation rates in nonagricultural pursuits. Where a trend
as such is pronounced in any one urban group, it will naturally
operate to reduce the average rate of female employment in that
group.

Variations in Female Responses to Economic Development

Up to this juncture the analysis has dealt with the
underdeveloped world as a group, or as sets of countries classified by rank order of development or urbanization. The danger
of such an approach is that it overshadows the considerable
variation that exists in women's nonagricultural participation
rates among countries characterized by a similar level of
economic development. The plausible notion that there may well
be differences in the response of the female labor force to
economic development has already been suggested by the discrepancy
between its historical evolution in the United States and in the
currently developing world. The testimony provided by individual
countries challenges the validity of a consistently positive
relationship between female employment rates in nonagricultural
pursuits and economic development level. In certain underdeveloped nations the female activity rates rise as high as 36
percent (Jamaica); in others they drop as low as 2 percent
(Pakistan). The range of this variation for twenty-eight underdeveloped countries is shown in Table 5. Because of the unequal
degree to which the developing world is industrialized, the

16

TABLE 5

FEMALE PARTICIPATION RATES, BY ACTIVITY RATE OF ADULT
MALES, IN NONAGRICULTURAL ECONOMIC ACTIVITIES
IN UNDERDEVELOPED COUNTRIES

Class and Country	Activity Rate		Population (millions)	
	Male	Female	Male	Female
Underdeveloped *(income/capita <U.S. $500)*				
Total	35.1	12.3	274.3	267.9
Class I: *male activity ranges from 40 to 56 percent*				
Chile	56.1	21.8	2.1	2.3
Portugal	48.2	14.0	2.9	3.4
Puerto Rico	46.2	19.7	0.7	0.7
Iraq	44.6	2.6	1.7	1.8
Greece	41.9	12.2	2.9	3.2
Costa Rica	40.9	16.3	0.3	0.4
Jamaica	40.5	35.7	0.5	0.5
Egypt	40.1	3.5	7.3	7.5
Rumania	40.0	12.6	6.2	6.8
Class II: *male activity ranges from 30 to <40 percent*				
Iran	39.6	7.0	5.6	5.4
Peru	39.5	15.3	2.8	2.9
Panama	38.6	23.3	0.3	0.3
Morocco	38.4	4.5	3.2	3.3
Turkey	36.4	2.7	8.2	8.1
Syria	35.0	3.2	1.2	1.2
Ecuador	34.9	21.8	1.2	1.3
Tunisia	34.9	4.4	1.1	0.9
India	31.9	8.8	133.6	125.2
Mexico	30.6	12.0	12.5	13.0
Class III: *male activity <30 percent*				
Nicaragua	29.4	19.0	0.4	0.4
Korea	29.1	9.1	7.3	8.1
El Salvador	28.1	17.4	0.7	0.7
Indonesia	26.9	10.9	27.0	28.7
Pakistan	26.4	2.3	26.6	23.5
Philippines	26.1	18.2	7.2	7.3
Honduras	23.9	13.1	0.5	0.5
Thailand	20.6	11.8	7.4	7.5
Sudan	14.6	1.6	2.9	3.0

Sources: See Table 1.

twenty-eight countries are grouped into developmental classes according to the activity rate of adult males in the nonagricultural sectors. The resultant rank order from which the classification of three developmental levels is derived is as follows: Class I countries represent the highest level of development: male activity rates range from 40 to 56 percent. In Class II countries the corresponding ratio ranges from 30 to less than 40 percent. Class III countries are the least developed economically: male activity rates outside the agricultural sector are less than 30 percent. Countries are listed in descending order of their developmental level. At one extreme are pre-industrial countries such as the Sudan and Thailand where male involvement outside the primary sector is minimal. At the other extreme are countries such as Chile where more than one-half of all adult males are engaged in economic activities unrelated to the agricultural sector.

A glance at the corresponding female activity rates in individual countries within and across development groups shows clearly *the inconsistent reaction of the female labor force to economic development*. In certain situations women's work participation does not respond at all to increasing development levels. Compare Class I countries such as Jamaica, Chile, Egypt, and Iraq. Despite the similarity in their developmental level, the female activity rates range from 36 percent in Jamaica, to 22 percent in Chile, to 3 percent in Egypt and Iraq. In other countries, by contrast, high rates of female participation are sustained independent of economic development. Compare Class III countries such as Nicaragua, the Philippines, and El Salvador, all of which are at the very early stage of industrial growth. Yet in these societies the female activity rates score as high as in Puerto Rico and in Chile, which are among the most developed countries on the list.

To determine whether such variations are typical only of developing countries, the dispersion in female activity rates was measured separately for the industrialized and for the underdeveloped countries included in Table 1. The results obtained read as follows: the mean female participation rate in nonagricultural pursuits in the industrialized countries is 28.1 percent, with a standard deviation of 5.4. With the exception of the United Kingdom, Denmark, and Germany, which rank rather high, and Venezuela, the Netherlands, and Israel, which score comparatively low, the remainder of the industrialized countries are close to the mean. By contrast, in the underdeveloped nations the female activity rates range from one to 36 percent, with a mean of 12.3 percent and a standard deviation of 8.0 (F ratio of 2.19 which is significant at $p < .05$). Obviously a host of factors other than the level of economic development is involved in determining the extent to which women

participate in economic activities outside of agriculture, at
least during the nascent period of industrialization.

A Comparison Between Latin American and Middle Eastern Countries

The uneven reaction of the nonagricultural female labor
force to the level of economic development is particularly
striking when female employment rates in Latin American and
Middle Eastern countries are compared. The disparity between
the two regions can be documented from the labor force data in
Table 5. The fact that these two regions are at roughly similar
stages of economic development and are characterized by different
social and cultural systems (Latin America is predominantly
Catholic, the Middle East predominantly Muslim) provides a unique
opportunity to examine more closely some aspects of the interre-
lationship among female employment patterns, social structure,
and economic development.

Table 6 shows ten Latin American and eight Middle Eastern
countries by level of economic development (as measured by male
activity rates in nonagricultural pursuits), the corresponding
rate of female participation, and the ratio of female workers in
the total nonagricultural labor force. Again the striking regional differences in women's work participation appear despite the
similarities in the level of economic development. In both
regions the average of activity rates of adult males in nonagricultural pursuits is 37 percent. By contrast, the corresponding
average of the female rates is nearly 20 percent in Latin America
but less than 4 percent in the Middle East. And whereas in Latin
America the ratio female in the total nonagricultural labor force
is 1:3, in the Middle East it is below 1:10. *The female activity
rate in the least developed country in Latin America--Honduras--
is six times as high as the female activity rate of the most developed country in the Middle East--Iraq.*

The most significant finding in Table 6 is the systematic
failure of women in all Middle Eastern countries to respond to
higher levels of economic development by a parallel increase in
participation rates. According to our indicator, Iraq is the
most advanced country in the Middle East, but the female activity
rate in Iraq is as low as it is in Pakistan, the least developed
country in that region.

Evidently, the behavior of Middle Eastern women represents
a strong deviation not only from the historical experience of the
now-industrialized West but also from the current experience of
the other countries undergoing industrialization.

The contrast in women's work participation between Middle
Eastern and non-Middle Eastern countries located at a similar

19

TABLE 6

LATIN AMERICAN AND MIDDLE EASTERN COMPARATIVE DIFFERENCES
IN FEMALE NONAGRICULTURAL LABOR FORCE: SELECTED
COUNTRIES GROUPED BY DEVELOPMENTAL LEVEL

(Data for population 15+)

Region and Country	Participation Rate		Female Percent of Total
	Male	Female	
Latin America			
Chile	56.1	21.8	30.6
Puerto Rico	46.2	19.7	31.0
Costa Rica	40.9	16.3	28.9
Jamaica	40.5	35.7	50.2
Peru	39.5	15.3	28.7
Ecuador	34.9	21.8	30.7
Mexico	30.6	12.0	26.3
Nicaragua	29.4	19.0	41.2
El Salvador	28.1	17.4	40.2
Honduras	23.9	13.1	36.4
Average	37.0	19.2	34.3
Middle East			
Iraq	44.6	2.6	5.5
Egypt	40.1	3.5	8.1
Iran	39.6	7.0	14.6
Morocco	38.4	4.5	10.9
Turkey	36.4	2.7	8.1
Syria	35.0	3.2	8.2
Tunisia	34.9	4.4	9.5
Pakistan	26.4	2.3	7.1
Average	37.0	3.7	9.0

Sources: See Table 1.

20

level of economic development is, indeed, striking. By eliminating
the Middle Eastern countries from the sets of countries ranked by
degree of urbanization in Table 3, the average of the female activity rates rises from 12 to 18 percent in Class I countries; from 15
to 19 percent in Class II; from 11 to 20.4 percent in Class III;
and from 10.6 to 16 percent in Class IV.

By contrast, Latin American women have the highest activity
rates reported among all the underdeveloped countries included in
Table 1. In fact, their activity rates remain high independent of
the particular level of economic development. For example, female
employment outside of agriculture in Nicaragua and in Ecuador is
almost as high as it is in the industrialized nations of the Netherlands, Norway, and Israel. Similarly, the female activity rates in
underdeveloped Jamaica parallel those reported for highly advanced
countries such as Sweden, Switzerland, and Denmark (Table 1).

Case Studies for Particular Analysis

It must be amply clear by now that the level of economic
development does not explain the extent to which women participate
in the nonagricultural labor force. To be able to understand more
closely the significant differential between Middle Eastern and
Latin American women in their response to economic development,
the thrust of the remaining part of this study is directed toward
an intensive analysis of thirteen countries within these two regions: Chile, Mexico, Ecuador, Colombia, Costa Rica, and Peru in
Latin America, Egypt, Morocco, Syria, Libya, Iran, Pakistan, and
Turkey in the Middle East.

The general level of differences between the two regions
shows up equally well in the sample of the countries selected.
In the Latin American context, the female activity percentage
rates in nonagricultural economic activities are: Chile, 21.8;
Ecuador, 21.8; Colombia, 18.1; Costa Rica, 16.3; Peru, 15.3; and
Mexico, 12.0. The corresponding percentage ratios for the Middle
Eastern countries are considerably lower: Iran, 7.0; Morocco,
4.5; Egypt, 3.5; Syria, 3.2; Libya, 3.0; Turkey, 2.7; and Pakistan, 2.3.

In terms of their regional representativeness, the countries selected for this study cover the entire range of variation.
With reference to Latin America, Chile represents a country in
which female participation rates are higher than the average;
Mexico ranks considerably below the mean-percent for the region,
and the other four countries are close to the average. Similarly, in the Middle East, Iran has the highest female employment
rate, Turkey and Pakistan the lowest, with all other countries
typical of the average.

21

Chapter 3

THE STRUCTURE OF THE FEMALE NONAGRICULTURAL LABOR FORCE

The limitations of invoking the level of economic development to explain the extent to which women participate in the nonagricultural labor force are now clear. The contrasting experience
of women workers in Latin America and in the Middle East has demonstrated unmistakably that the female response to similar levels
of economic development is by no means uniform. We are now in a
position to take this finding a step further by inquiring if the
striking differentials in female employment rates between the
Latin American and the Middle Eastern countries can be accounted
for by regional differences in the structure of demand for workers.

Countries at a similar level of economic development may
differ with respect to the specific organization of their economy.
This may create differences in the work opportunities available
to both men and women in the labor market. For example, economies that specialize in light industries, such as textiles, tobacco, food and beverages, tend to prefer women workers. Where
the focus is on heavy industries, women are more or less excluded.
It is conceivable, therefore, that the low feminine employment
rates in Middle Eastern countries inhere in the particular structure of the nonagricultural economy which may not be conducive to
providing occupational opportunities for women in the labor market. In an attempt to explain the regional differences between
the Latin American and the Middle Eastern countries, two separate
enquiries suggest themselves. First, are there basic differences
in the specific organization of the nonagricultural economy between the two regions which could cause variations in the structure of demand for female workers? Second, if the first answer
is negative, how else can the regional disparity in women's
response to a similar labor market condition be explained?

The Structure of Demand for Workers in the Labor Market

Tables 7 and 8 present a detailed breakdown of the industrial and occupational structure of the total nonagricultural
labor force in the thirteen countries under study. The distribution of manpower among the different occupations and industries
reflects the specific organization of the economy in each country.

TABLE 7

DISTRIBUTION BY ECONOMIC BRANCH OF ACTIVITY OF TOTAL NONAGRICULTURAL LABOR FORCE IN SELECTED
COUNTRIES IN LATIN AMERICA AND THE MIDDLE EAST

(Population 15+, c. 1960)

Regions and Countries	All Industries Total (100 percent)[a]	Industries						
		Extractive	Manufacturing	Construction	Electricity and Gas	Commerce	Transport	Public and Administrative Services
Latin America								
Chile[b]	1,578,427	5.8	27.2	8.6	1.2	15.3	7.8	34.5
Colombia	2,460,197	3.2	26.2	8.9	0.5	17.6	7.8	35.8
Costa Rica[b]	195,456	0.6	23.2	11.9	2.2	19.8	7.5	34.8
Ecuador	572,558	0.6	35.4	8.1	0.5	15.8	7.3	32.3
Mexico[b]	5,106,685	2.8	30.5	7.9	0.8	21.1	7.0	29.9
Peru	1,404,040	4.7	29.0	7.4	0.6	19.9	6.7	31.6
Average		2.9	28.6	8.8	1.0	18.2	7.2	33.1
Middle East								
Egypt	3,154,860	0.7	22.3	5.0	1.2	20.0	8.1	42.8
Iran	3,283,917	0.8	32.9	15.0	1.6	16.4	6.7	26.6
Libya	195,802	5.9	12.9	15.3	2.8	12.6	11.0	39.4
Morocco	1,011,416	3.9	26.3	5.6	0.8	23.6	7.9	31.9
Pakistan	7,309,698	0.3	33.6	4.7	0.5	20.2	7.2	33.5
Syria	419,445	0.9	26.9	12.3	1.6	19.9	8.7	29.6
Turkey	2,939,551	2.9	32.7	11.9	0.9	13.3	9.8	28.4
Average		2.2	26.8	9.9	1.3	18.0	8.5	33.1

[a]Totals may not sum to 100 because of rounding. Computations exclude all economically active population classified in "Ill Defined" and "Unknown" categories.

[b]Population 12 and over.

Sources: Chile, 1964:Table 24; Colombia, 1967:Table 36; Costa Rica, 1966:Table 13; Ecuador, 1964:
Table 10; Mexico, 1962:Table 25; Peru, 1964:Table 91; Egypt, 1963:Table 4; Iran, 1964:
Table 21; Libya, 1966:Tables 49, 51; Morocco, undated:Table 27; Syria, 1962:Table 37;
Turkey, 1969:Table 42; UN, 1968:Table 2A.

TABLE 8

OCCUPATIONAL DISTRIBUTION OF THE NONAGRICULTURAL LABOR FORCE IN SELECTED COUNTRIES
IN LATIN AMERICA AND THE MIDDLE EAST
(Population 15+, c. 1960)

Region and Country	All Occupations[a] (100 percent)	Professional	Administrative/ Managerial	Clerical	Sales	Workers, Mines	Workers, Transport/ Communication	Craftsmen/ Workers, Production Processes	Service, Sport, and Recreation
Latin America									
Chile	1,583,785	7.6	2.9	10.2	10.6	3.5	4.9	40.1	20.3
Colombia	2,528,994	7.9	5.3	9.4	11.4	1.7	6.1	35.4	22.7
Costa Rica[b]	189,105	10.9	2.7	10.9	15.8	0.6	4.8	33.9	19.9
Ecuador[b]	583,667	7.7	0.6	7.9	14.6	0.4	5.0	40.2	17.2
Mexico[b]	5,256,896	7.8	1.8	13.2	19.5	2.1	←——— 40.8 ———→		14.9
Peru	1,399,763	7.3	3.2	9.5	16.0	2.5	5.0	38.7	17.6
Average		8.1	2.7	10.1	14.6	1.8	5.1	38.1	18.7
Middle East									
Egypt	3,044,347	7.1	2.5	8.5	18.2	0.4	6.8	36.0	21.0
Iran	3,177,322	6.4	0.4	6.3	15.6	↕	57.3	→|	14.0
Morocco	1,135,200	8.6	1.3	5.5	16.4	3.1	5.0	37.0	23.1
Libya	195,264	6.0	2.8	9.5	11.9	3.5	10.1	36.0	19.8
Pakistan	7,138,637	5.8	1.9	7.6	18.2	0.3	6.2	45.8	14.3
Syria	417,398	5.2	1.3	7.1	19.1	0.7	7.5	48.2	10.9
Turkey	3,380,592	9.2	←——— 10.9 ———→		11.5	1.9	8.5	45.5	13.0
Average		6.9	1.5	7.4	15.8	1.6	7.3	41.4	16.6

[a]Totals may not sum to 100 because of rounding. Computations exclude all economically active population classified in "Ill Defined" and "Unknown" categories.
[b]Population 12 and older.

Sources: Chile, 1964:Table 3.4; Colombia, 1967:Table 38; Costa Rica, 1966:Table 35; Ecuador, 1964: Table 10; Mexico, 1962:Table 26; Peru, 1964:Table 85; Egypt, 1963:Table 32; Iran, 1968:Table 16; Libya, 1966:Table 41; Morocco, undated:Table 30; Syria, 1962:Table 44; Turkey, 1969:Table 30; UN, 1968: Table 2B.

These distribution patterns are, in turn, expected to indicate whether or not basic differences exist in the structure of demand for workers between the Latin American and the Middle Eastern regions.

As can be seen from these tables, there is considerable uniformity between the two areas with respect to the particular pattern of distribution of the total nonagricultural labor force throughout the industrial sectors and the occupational categories. When the average of each region is computed, the proportion of manpower allotted to each branch of economic activity is virtually identical. This is true for both industries and services. For example, both Middle Eastern and Latin American countries earmark approximately the same proportion of their labor force to the manufacturing industries, to construction, to commerce, to transport, and to public and administrative services. Although there are individual country differences within each region (and this is particularly more striking in the Middle East than it is in Latin America), the range of this variation is minimal (Table 7).

With respect to the distribution of the nonagricultural labor force within specific occupational categories, the only apparent difference between the two regions falls within the clerical and transportation categories. Latin American countries have a relatively higher percentage of manpower invested in nonprofessional white-collar employment than the Middle East; the inverse is true for manual labor related to transportation. Insofar as all the other occupational categories are concerned--the professions, sales, production process workers, artisans and operatives, and the services--the proportion of workers employed in each specific occupational grouping shows surprising uniformity between the two regions (Table 8).

The similarity in the structure of the total nonagricultural labor force that has thus far been shown to exist between the Latin American and the Middle Eastern countries eliminates the possibility that variations in labor market demands are at the root of the female differential in employment rates. The thrust of the remaining part of this chapter is directed toward offering an alternative interpretation of the female differences in labor force behavior between the two regions. Basically, it is argued that in the particular countries under study female employment rates depend in large part upon the interplay between two forces: the particular reaction of women to the labor market situation, and the occupational opportunities actually available to them in the labor market. Both these conditions are intimately related to the cultural definition within a society regarding the type of work deemed appropriate for women. Viewed from this perspective, it will be shown that in Middle Eastern societies female participation rates may actually have little to do with *either* the level of economic development *or* the structure of demand for workers in the labor market.

This proposition will be substantiated by using two types of analysis. First is a regional comparison of the composition of the female labor force for the purpose of establishing systematic differences in the patterning of the two populations. The second line of analysis involves an interpretation of these differences, with a view to demonstrating how the latter have a meaningful bearing on explaining the disparity in female employment rates between the Latin American and Middle Eastern countries.

Patterns of Differences in the Structure of the Female Labor Force

One of the striking contrasts between Latin American and Middle Eastern countries occurs in the structure of female employment in the nonagricultural sectors of the economy. This contrast is particularly significant because countries in these two regions display basic similarities in the specific organization of their economy.

The low level of female involvement in the Middle Eastern societies leads to a natural expectation of a considerably less equitable sex distribution in all the industrial and occupational sectors. However, a systematic under-representation of women in specific employment sectors is decisive for the Middle East. This under-representation points, in turn, to a distinctive sex-segregated division of labor in that region. The consistency of the pattern becomes increasingly evident when one considers, by specific occupation and industry group, the proportion of the total economically active population who are female (Table 9). If there is no sex discrimination in employment situations, women are expected to furnish the same ratio of workers in each sector as they supply to the labor force as a whole. The fact that in the Middle Eastern countries this ratio is not approximated in specific occupational and industrial sectors, whereas in the Latin American countries it is, emphasizes some of the more important differences between feminine employment patterns in the two regions. It also explains why female participation in Middle Eastern societies is reduced below levels that otherwise would obtain.

Let us attempt a breakdown of this situation with the purpose of coming to grips with the salient factors that underlie its structure.

The Absence of Middle Eastern Women from Service Occupations.--In the experience of the now-industrialized nations, service occupations have been among women's top income-earning activities during the early period of economic development [Davis, 1958:78]. One of the major reasons for this trend is the rapid

26

TABLE 9

SPECIFIC OCCUPATIONAL CATEGORY AND INDUSTRIAL ACTIVITY BRANCH OF FEMALE PROPORTION OF TOTAL NON-AGRICULTURAL ECONOMICALLY ACTIVE POPULATION: SELECTED LATIN AMERICAN AND MIDDLE EASTERN COUNTRIES

Region and Country	Occupations						Industries							
	ALL OCCUPATIONS	Professions	White Collar	Sales	Manual Labor	Service (inc, domestic)	ALL INDUSTRIES	Extractive	Manufacturing	Construction	Electricity and Gas	Commerce	Transport	Public & Administrative
Latin America														
Chile	31.0	50.0	28.0	28.4	14.0	70.0	30.6	1.8	23.7	0.6	4.4	24.3	5.4	--
Colombia	34.2	47.3	50.4	25.5	69.8	74.5	33.9	24.6	27.3	1.6	7.6	24.8	6.4	58.5
Costa Rica	31.2	56.1	28.1	18.8	50.2	68.8	30.8	1.3	23.6	1.4	5.0	17.8	4.3	60.8
Ecuador	32.9	48.5	30.3	23.0	36.3	68.7	32.0	5.8	32.5	1.6	--	23.4	2.8	51.4
Mexico	28.2	38.0	30.0	28.5	15.0	66.0	26.5	6.8	16.0	3.5	9.4	27.0	5.3	--
Peru	30.1	46.2	46.2	28.9	41.7	60.0	29.5	2.7	28.1	0.9	4.5	28.0	4.9	48.1
Middle East														
Egypt	7.4	22.6	4.5	5.5	3.0	16.0	7.4	0.3	3.3	0.3	0.7	15.9	0.9	9.2
Iran	17.3	25.6	5.7	1.0	21.7	20.6	16.5	1.4	36.5	0.3	1.3	1.6	1.1	17.2
Libya (citizens)	6.0	11.5	1.9	0.7	11.5	5.5	6.2	0.4	28.1	0.5	1.3	0.8	0.5	5.8
Morocco														
All women	17.1	14.8	28.8	4.0	21.8	27.4	18.5	0.8	30.0	0.4	16.0	6.0	0.3	37.2
Muslim women	13.6	4.8	3.5	2.0	19.0	24.3	14.3	1.5	31.6	0.3	0.9	4.5	1.1	27.5
Pakistan	7.0	7.8	1.0	2.2	50.0	30.0	7.3	1.1	10.5	1.3	--	2.0	0.5	6.6
Syria (Arab women)	7.2	27.3	11.0	0.5	14.0	14.4	7.1	0.1	6.6	1.0	1.1	1.1	0.9	16.6
Turkey (Turkish women)	8.7	19.5	12.6	1.3	13.6	7.2	7.1	1.3	8.1	0.5	1.7	5.0	2.1	12.4

Sources: For occupational category data, see source note to Table 8; for industrial activity data see source note to Table 7.

rate of urbanization and its supply of a large number of women
who are marginal in relation to constructive employment. Since
service-type jobs require no specialized training outside that
received in the home, it is easy to see how such occupations
become the logical outlet when economic necessity requires women
to work.

Women have found domestic service, in particular, to be
functional in many ways. Although this activity is carried on
outside the home, it is possible to combine family responsibilities
with domestic service work in private households. During the
early period of industrialization, when the female labor force
was not yet emancipated from its undifferentiated state, and the
separation of the home and work place was not fully accepted,
domestic service was particularly convenient because it allowed
women to transfer some of their family responsibilities to their
place of employment [Stycos and Weller, 1967:219].

The Latin American countries conform to this experience
of feminine employment patterns in the Western nations as witnessed by the high participation rates reported for their women
in the service occupations. According to the occupational statistics, in all but Peru, women comprise close to 70 percent of all
workers classified in the service category. The preponderance
of Latin American women in this type of work is also reflected
in the cross-classification of industrial statistics by occupation groupings, which points to the considerable number of women
in service-type jobs within the different branches of economic
activity.

Mexico serves as an illustrative example. In that country
women comprise 43 percent of *all* service workers (excluding
domestic service) employed in the public and administrative
services sector. In the industry sectors the proportion of female workers among all service workers is very high in the manufacturing branches (63 percent) and in construction (55 percent).
In the extractive and the electricity and gas industries, approximately one worker in every three employed in some service-type
job is a woman.

In Latin America the high female representation in the
service occupations is boosted by the domestic service category,
which, in almost all of the countries in that region, is virtually an exclusive female domain. Close to 90 percent of all
domestic servants in Chile, 80 percent in Colombia, and 68 percent in each of Peru and Mexico are women.

In considering the experience of the Middle Eastern
countries, however, it becomes evident that the process of
modernization does not draw women automatically into service
occupations. In the seven Middle Eastern countries under study,

males dominate service occupations. According to the occupational statistics, the female proportion among all service workers ranges from as low as 5 percent (Libya and Turkey) to 15 percent (Syria and Egypt) to approximately 30 percent (Morocco and Pakistan). For the Middle East region as a whole, the average of the female ratio in service-type occupations is 16 percent; in Latin America it is 70 percent.

A decisive factor for the Middle East's low ratio is the relative absence of women from employment in domestic service. Although census information does not spell out domestic service as a separate occupational category (except in Morocco) domestic work in private households is included under such rubrics as "personal services" or "servants, cooks, and housekeepers." In either case the proportion of female workers is minimal. For example, the female ratio of *all* housekeepers, cooks, and maids is only 17 percent in Syria and 10 percent in Turkey. In Libya, among workers classified in the personal services, only 10 percent are female.

Morocco is the only Middle Eastern country which deviates from the norm. Relative to all other countries in the region, the proportion of Moroccan women represented in the service occupations is high. This is accounted for almost entirely by a large-scale involvement in domestic service--55 percent--and in housekeeping jobs--28 percent. More than 50 percent of all domestic service jobs and 80 percent of all housekeeper jobs are in female hands. In Morocco the other two occupational groupings which claim a relatively high proportion of female workers are cooks (35 percent) and laundry workers (60 percent).

Middle Eastern women also avoid systematically the non-domestic service occupations available in the different branches of economic activity. Such jobs are predominantly male.

In Egypt, for example, the lower-ranking service occupations account for 30 percent of all the male workers employed in the public and administrative services sector, but only for 7 percent of the female workers. Numerically, the marginal services represent the second largest occupational grouping for male workers in the public and administrative services sector. There are 2.5 times as many men employed in menial service jobs as in the professions and three times as many as in clerical jobs.

By contrast, the proportion of Egyptian women involved in menial service jobs in the public and administrative services sector represents approximately one-ninth of the women who are employed in a professional capacity.

Another way of underlining the minimal participation of Middle Eastern women in service-type activities is to contrast

29

the situations obtaining in Egypt and Mexico. Whereas Mexican women comprise between 30 and 40 percent of all service workers in the services sector of the economy and 60 percent of all service workers in the manufacturing branches, in Egypt the corresponding female ratio among all workers in these two sectors is *one percent* (see Appendix Table 1).

Factory Work: Taboo for Middle Eastern Women

One other significant contrast between the Latin American and Middle Eastern occupational structures concerns female participation in factory work. The Latin American countries report a substantial number of female factory workers, the Middle Eastern countries virtually none.

In Egypt, Syria, and Turkey, women's absence from the factory is reflected in their insignificant proportion among the economically active population engaged in the manufacturing industries (industrial statistics) and among "artisans engaged in production process" category (occupational statistics). For example, among every 100 workers in the manufacturing branches, only three in Egypt, seven in Syria, and eight in Turkey are women. But, in Morocco, Libya, Pakistan, and Iran, the figures on female participation in the industries are considerably higher; however, the majority of these female workers are engaged in cottage-type industry production in or near the home. Furthermore, their productive role is limited to handicrafts, embroidery, needlework, pottery making, and traditional spinning and weaving. The number of Moroccan, Libyan, and Pakistani women actually engaged in factory-type production is minimal.

It can, of course, be argued that in these three countries industrial production in general has not shifted to the factory. Nevertheless, a closer examination of the class of worker statistics in those countries shows that despite the prevalence of traditional manufacturing, women definitely avoid factory work. For example, the class of workers statistics shows a considerable sex discrepancy in the number of industry workers who are self employed, who are unpaid family labor, and who are salaried and/or wage earners. Only the third group is considered to be working under factory conditions.[1] Thus, for example, the percentage among all male workers engaged in the manufacturing industries and categorized as self employed or unpaid workers is 40 percent in Morocco, 65 percent in Pakistan, and 26 percent in Libya. The corresponding ratios for the women workers in these three countries are respectively 60, 94, and 90 percent. (See Appendix Table 2.)

---

[1]For definition of cottage industries, refer to Jaffe and Azumi [1960].

In Egypt, Syria, and Turkey, two major reasons account for the absence of women from the manufacturing industries: women have not been associated with handicraft production (which means they play no role in the traditional manufacturing branches), and they do not participate in factory work. The Egyptian women's lack of participation in traditional handicrafts is so marked that the Lacoutures observed: "With few exceptions the womenfolk have forgotten any form of artisan work or craftsmanship. They neither spin nor weave; they cannot embroider or sew" [Lacouture, 1958: 383].

The absence of women from household industries is substantiated by the Egyptian and Syrian statistics. In these two countries, among every 100 workers in the manufacturing sector who are operating under cottage-type industry production, the proportion of women workers is less than 5 percent. Insofar as factory-type production is concerned, the female proportion among all the salaried or wage-earning workers is only 5 percent in Egypt and 6 percent in Syria despite close to 80 percent of all manufacturing production having shifted to the factory. Furthermore, Syria and Egypt specialize in light manufacturing, particularly textiles, in which women workers are generally competitive with men.

The absence of Middle Eastern women from the industrial sector is best demonstrated in Table 10, where the manufacturing branches are broken down into the various industry groups. The importance of the female component in each industry is measured by proportion. As can be seen, all industry sectors, except for tobacco manufacturing and textiles, are almost exclusively male domains.

In Latin American countries, by contrast, the female participation in industrial production is substantial, as evidenced by the number of women reported in the manufacturing branches (industrial statistics) and in the production-process worker category (occupational statistics). First of all, females in those countries average 25 percent of all workers in the manufacturing branches, the proportion being highest in Ecuador and lowest in Mexico. Second, among workers engaged in the production process an average of three in ten are women. Furthermore, women outnumber male workers in industries related to apparel and to fur and leather wear; they predominate heavily in the textiles, and comprise between 25 and 35 percent of all those engaged in the tobacco, paper, and chemical industries, and in food processing. In Peru, women are also heavily represented in industrial activities related to packing and labeling.

In most Latin American countries the home industries play a relatively minor role in industrial production, and where

31

TABLE 10

FEMALE PROPORTION OF MANUFACTURING SECTOR WORKERS
BY TYPE OF INDUSTRY: LATIN AMERICA
AND THE MIDDLE EAST
(Population 15+)

Industry Group	Chile[a]	Colombia	Egypt	Syria	Turkey
All manufacturing industries	24.0	27.0	3.3	6.5	8.1
Food	12.5	22.8	2.3	3.3	4.8
Beverages	7.7	10.3	1.1	2.1	5.8
Tobacco	31.7	56.4	1.5	46.3	51.5
Textiles	38.0	52.4	4.7	11.5	21.9
Wearing apparel, footwear and other textiles	61.0	60.0	1.8	6.9	6.1
Wood (except furniture)	2.4	9.6	0.4	0.6	1.1
Furniture and fixtures	3.5	5.1	0.1	0.3	1.3
Paper and allied products	15.0	24.8	5.0	0.7	11.3
Printing, publishing and related	14.0	20.2	0.4	1.5	4.0
Leather and leather products	10.1	13.0	1.2	0.9	0.9
Rubber products	13.0	15.4	2.3	5.1	6.3
Chemicals and chemical products	21.7	28.7	4.4	3.7	12.7
Petroleum and coal products	0.1	8.2	1.3	1.7	4.3
Nonmetallic products (except petroleum and coal)	7.9	10.7	1.6	1.5	3.6
Metal smelting, basic metal and metal products	5.5	12.8	0.9	0.9	1.0
Machinery	3.5	3.7	0.4	0.5	1.5
Electrical machinery, equipment, appliances	10.0	6.8	1.0	0.0	3.5
Repair of transport equipment	1.7	1.8	0.2	0.0	3.8
Miscellaneous	9.0	23.4	21.0	10.8	9.7

[a]Population 12+.

Sources: Chile, 1964:Table 3.5.2; Colombia, 1967:Table 37;
Egypt, 1963:Table 14; Syria, 1962:Table 34; Turkey,
1969:Table 42.

they do prevail, there is no indication that female involvement
is any heavier than male. The class of worker statistics shows
that the typical female worker is employed under factory-type
conditions. In addition, there is little sex differential between the proportion of industry workers who are salaried or wage
earners and those who are self employed or unpaid workers. In
the manufacturing branches of industrial production, the percentage of all women workers who are salaried or wage earners is 66
percent in Costa Rica, 60 percent in Ecuador, 64 percent in
Chile, and 76 percent in Mexico. The corresponding percentages
for the male workers are 82, 60, 75, and 74 percent, respectively.

Activities Related to Trade: A Male Domain in the Middle East

Latin American and Middle Eastern countries differ considerably also with respect to women's participation in activities
related to trade and to sales. In countries experiencing the
early phases of industrialization and urbanization, women are
expected to derive handsome advantages from income-earning activities related to petty trade, retail, and door-to-door sales.
First of all, in countries where the department store has not
yet replaced the bazaar, petty trade and retail is one other
marginal-type occupation (besides domestic service) which is
particularly suited to women who have no specialized training yet
are in need of work. In addition, such activities do not fall
under regular employment conditions as do domestic service or
factory work. They can be carried on informally, at irregular
hours, and oftentimes near the woman's home, all of which incentives create an opportunity for women with families to combine
an income-earning activity with household responsibilities.

Evidently, Latin American women have taken advantage of
the opportunities offered by this type of work. Middle Eastern
women, by contrast, have shied away from the trade sector and
from the sales occupations, leaving them almost exclusively as
male domains.

According to the industrial classification, in Latin
America, on the average, *one worker in four* engaged in the
trade/commerce sector is female; in the Middle East, the corresponding proportion is one-fifth as much--*one woman in twenty
workers*. A glance at the occupational statistics emphasizes
the regional differences even more strongly. Among all workers
who are employed in occupations related to sales, one in four
is a woman in Latin America compared to one in fifty in the
Middle East. In countries such as Libya, Syria, and Turkey, the
female ratio in the sales category is barely one percent; in
Morocco, among Muslim female workers, the ratio is 2 percent,
and in Egypt it is 5 percent. In fact, it is only in Egypt and
Morocco that female involvement in petty trade and in retail is

33

somewhat discernible. In Morocco the women classified in the
trade sector are mostly salesgirls, but then again, one-half of
them are foreigners. In Turkey the few women who are classified
in the commerce/trade sector are connected with insurance, real
estate, or other financial institutions; hardly *any* among them
are salesgirls.

Preference for the Professions Among Middle Eastern Women

Thus far the discussion has centered around the low-level
occupations which draw their resources from the least-educated
and presumably the most tradition-bound segment of the population.
Let us turn now to examine women's work participation in upgraded
occupations such as the professions and white collar jobs. Since
in developing countries female education is generally associated
with socio-economic status, it is expected that women involved in
upgraded occupations reflect the behavior of the more privileged
social groups of their societies.

A glance at Table 9 indicates that in both Latin America
and the Middle East women are highly represented in professional
occupations. This is not meant to imply, however, that a similarity in the pattern of female participation in the professions
exists between the two regions. In fact, the reverse is true.
In the Latin American countries, one professional position in
every two is in female hands; in the Middle East, the corresponding proportion is only one in six, when resident foreign women
are included in the count, and one in seven when only Middle
Eastern women are considered. This regional imbalance should
not, however, lead us to overlook the fact that educated women
in the Middle East show a very high propensity for employment
in professional fields.

One way of assessing the importance of the professions
as far as female employment in the Middle East is concerned,
is to compare the female ratio in the professions with the female proportion of workers in the nonagricultural labor force as
a whole. In this respect one can say that women in Syria furnish
four times as many workers to the professions as they do to the
total work force, Egyptian women three times as many, and Libyan
and Turkish women twice as many. In fact, Morocco is the only
Middle Eastern country in which the contribution of women to the
professions is equal to the female ratio in the labor force as a
whole.

The emphasis placed upon female employment in the professions can also be assessed from the occupational distribution
of the female labor force. In the Middle East, one out of four
women in the labor force is employed in a professional capacity.
This ratio does not obtain in the Latin American countries,

despite their higher female educational standards, because educated Latin American women are distributed fairly evenly between
professional and nonprofessional white-collar occupations. For
example, in Latin America among the total number of women workers
in nonagricultural occupations, 12 percent are engaged in clerical and other white-collar type occupations, whereas in the
Middle East the female concentration in the upgraded occupations
is almost exclusively in professional categories. A comparison
between Mexico and Egypt will serve to illustrate these regional
differences more concretely.

In Mexico the cross-classification of the female labor
force by industry and occupation indicates that for every 100
women employed in the public and administrative services sector,
38 are in clerical and administrative jobs and 45 are in the
professions, as compared to male workers among whom the corresponding distribution reads 50 and 30 percent respectively. In
Egypt, by contrast, among every 100 women employed in the same
sector, only *eight* are reported in clerical and administrative
employment and sixty are in the professions. Conversely, among
Egyptian men, 50 percent are involved in clerical/administrative
type jobs and 8 percent are holding professional positions.

The numerical preponderance of Latin American and Middle
Eastern women in the professions should not, however, divert us
from observing that both societies rigidly confine these women
to two subprofessional categories: school teaching and nursing.
The relegation of women to these two fields is particularly
strong in the Middle East where females are virtually excluded
from participation in any other professional specialization.

Not all of the countries under study provide cross-
classified data regarding professional workers by field of
specialization and by sex. The rigidity of the occupational
structure can nevertheless be substantiated in the case of
Egypt, Syria, Libya, Chile, and Mexico.

In the three Middle Eastern countries, teaching absorbs
close to 40 percent of all professional female workers; nursing
and teaching combined account for 96 percent. In Chile and
Mexico the female concentration around these two subprofessions
is admittedly also high. However, women there have *begun* to
break through the barrier somewhat more successfully. In Chile,
for example, one in five women reported to be holding professional
jobs is involved in fields outside of teaching and nursing.
According to Chilean 1960 figures, there were 1,200 female
doctors (18 percent of the total), 1,200 female chemists (39
percent) and 200 women specialized in mathematics and in the
sciences (18 percent).

35

The diversification of Latin American women into various fields of professional specialization is also reflected in the substantial number of women employed in a professional capacity in the different branches of the economy. In Mexico, for example, women monopolize one-half of all the professional positions in the public and administrative sector, one-fourth in the commerce sector, and one-fifth in the industrial branches related to manufacturing. In Egypt, by contrast, all professional female workers are concentrated in public and administrative services since this sector absorbs the nursing and teaching professions. Professional positions in all the other branches of the national economy and, with the exception of teaching and nursing, in the public and administrative services sector are exclusively male domains.

Clerical Occupations in the Middle East: A Male Stronghold

Table 9 shows the marked differences between the nonagricultural female labor forces in Latin America and the Middle East with respect to women's participation in nonprofessional white collar occupations. Typically, in Latin America one-third of all clerical and administrative positions are ceded to women; in the Middle East, by contrast, the corresponding ratio is one woman among every ten workers. Moreover, when (as in Morocco) foreign women are separated from the count, the average female ratio among all clerical and administrative workers in the Middle East is reduced to 6 percent—one in seventeen.

Middle Eastern countries are noted for manning their elaborate bureaucratic networks with men, from the bottom rungs of the clerical and administrative ladder to the top echelons. In individual Middle Eastern countries among every 100 workers engaged in clerical/administrative work, the proportion who are female is one percent each in Pakistan and Libya and 4 percent in Egypt. In Turkey and in Syria the female ratio is considerably larger: approximately 11 and 12 percent respectively. Even then, Turkish and Syrian women lag far behind their counterparts in Latin America. In countries such as Chile, Ecuador, and Mexico, approximately 30 percent of all manpower engaged in clerical and administrative-type employment is female. In Costa Rica and Peru the female ratio in this particular occupational category is even higher: 38 and 42 percent respectively.

Seclusion Patterns Among Female Workers in the Middle East

An attempt has been made thus far to identify patterns of difference between the female labor force in Latin American and Middle Eastern countries. It is possible now to assume an

36

interpretive stance by relating these differences to the broader
social context in which female labor force participation takes
place.

We have noted how, despite regional similarities in the
structure of demand for workers, women in Latin America and in
the Middle East have reacted to the labor market situation in
strikingly different ways. In the Middle Eastern context the
differences displayed point systematically to one major direction:
female workers there show a distinctively strong seclusion pattern
in the sense that they avoid occupational sectors which involve
public activity or presuppose contact with men. When the rare
Middle Eastern woman does take the risk, she concentrates on
income-earning activities, such as home industries and the
teaching profession, which guarantee a conservative atmosphere
with a minimum possibility of intermingling with the opposite
sex.

Of course, what is theoretically decisive here from the
economic development point of view is that in the Middle Eastern
world the advent of industrialization has not led women to enter
into the industrial and commercial markets traditionally associated with female employment. As a consequence, occupations which
in other countries become predominantly feminine from early industrialization onwards (such as the service occupations, domestic
work, factory work, retail, and clerical jobs) are in the Middle
East staffed by men or by foreign women (as in Morocco).

Reference was made earlier to the relationship between
female employment patterns and the cultural definition within a
society regarding the type of work deemed appropriate for women
to pursue. Viewed from this perspective, it is argued that the
absence of Middle Eastern women from occupational sectors historically associated with female employment can be understood as
a result of the interplay between women's avoidance of certain
sectors, because of the socially stigmatizing aspect, and the
informal prohibition of occupational opportunities imposed by
males. The former acts as a volitional seclusion, the latter
as an imposed exclusion. The reasons why such patterns prevail
and the mechanisms by which they are upheld are dealt with in
later chapters. The focus of the present discussion is directed
toward establishing a connection between the distinctive
patterning of the female labor force behavior in the Middle East
and the seclusion ethics prevalent in those societies.

Unfortunately, it is difficult to document the exact
interplay between seclusion and exclusion patterns in the Middle
East because of the disjunction between official hiring policy,
which in most Middle Eastern countries does not discriminate
by sex, and the social stigmatizing aspect which penalizes
women who threaten to violate morality taboos. The exclusion

imposed by men is informal; nevertheless, it is sufficiently powerful to enforce limitations upon the particular type of public activity available to women regardless of what the official stand
may be.

In our discussion we try to underline the ways and means
by which the combined effects of female seclusion and exclusion
operate in Middle Eastern countries to discourage women from en-
tering into certain occupational sectors. This is done by focusing the analysis upon those employment areas where the discrepancy
in female participation between the Middle Eastern and Latin
American countries has been shown to be the greatest, beginning
with the *service* occupations.

The low involvement of women in service-type occupations
in the Middle East is paradoxical unless the particular conditions
of work are considered. Female employment in domestic service,
it will be remembered, entails a displacement from the parental
or conjugal home to that of the employer, where the servant is
expected to reside and where she is brought into frequent and
unsupervised contact with men: male members of her employer's
family, male servants, and male strangers as well. In nondomestic service occupations, whether in hotels, restaurants, offices,
or factories, the woman is exposed even more closely to interaction with men since she is removed from almost all familial
supervision and control. Because in Middle Eastern societies
the intermingling of the sexes is generally viewed with suspicion,
and since the slightest doubts concerning the sex ethics of a
woman compromise her entire family, male guardians prevent their
womenfolk from joining service-type occupations. What is more,
women themselves tend to avoid such an employment area if they
can because of its highly compromising nature.

Given this framework, one can understand why in the Middle
East female employment in the factory is an equally sensitive
matter. The proximity of factory workers of both sexes gives
rise to fears of violating sex taboos: factory girls are considered "promiscuous" [Forget, 1962:107]. Although the mistrust
with which Middle Easterners view factory employment for women
can be documented, it is still not clear whether women shy away
from factory employment or whether they simply are not hired.

In Pakistan most factories are closed to women [Inter-
national Labor Review, 1953:315]. In Egypt the few textile
plants which employ female workers segregate the sexes and place
women under strict female supervision. Both cases point to the
external imposition of prohibitions and to the limitations of
occupational opportunities to women. In Morocco, however, there
is evidence of a strong stigma against female factory workers--a
stigma voiced by both sexes alike. A recent survey conducted in
that country to investigate the attitude of Moroccans toward

women's work indicated that both sexes linked female factory employment with promiscuity. They accused the female factory worker of taking on such jobs for "wanting to play around with men" [Forget, 1962:114]. If the sanctions against female factory work are as vehement in other Middle Eastern countries as in Morocco, it is highly improbable that women will take up such work even when employment is available.

Within the context of the combined effect of volitional seclusion and imposed exclusion it is also clear why in the Middle East all activities related to the trade sector and to sales occupations are deemed inappropriate for women. Whether such activities entail a small shop, a stand in the bazaar, door-to-door sales, or merely peddling, they all expose women to a vulnerable setting which can be highly stigmatized because it is broadly unsupervised and unstructured.

Although modernization in the Middle Eastern countries has favored including women in the professions, it has not had an equal impact upon their employment in white-collar positions. The near absence of Middle Eastern women from the ranks of clerical and related occupations is, in fact, a strong indicator that a decline in the traditional constraints imposed upon women is not an obligatory accompaniment of higher social status and educational achievement. From the striking sex differentials in the upgraded occupations, it is clear that even among the more privileged social groups Middle Eastern women are still discouraged from participating in employment sectors which presuppose contact with the opposite sex.

Table 9 showed that in the Middle East women's low involvement in clerical, administrative, and managerial positions has resulted in the masculinization of the entire network of the bureaucracy. An important cause of the persistently low female involvement in nonprofessional white collar jobs lies in the general prejudice against such employment because it fails to guarantee a secluded atmosphere. Whether a woman works as a private secretary, a switchboard operator, or an administrator she is exposed to the public eye. In such a situation, where outsiders can observe her in close contact with the opposite sex, morality taboos assume a great importance.

Until recently, clerical occupations in the Middle East, particularly those connected with foreign enterprises, embassies, and international organizations, were filled by non-Muslim women, either foreign nationals or members of religious minorities.[2]

---

[2]The resistance among Muslim women to clerical employment can be documented for Egypt where of the 480 women employed in the

These women enjoyed a freer social life and higher educational
standards than their Muslim counterparts. They learned foreign
languages in parochial schools and thus were able to take advantage of the commercial institutes established for the benefit of
the foreign communities. These factors combined to give foreign
and local Christian and Jewish girls early access to and consequent monopoly of most secretarial and other types of clerical
positions in the private sector. In time female white-collar
jobs were labeled as "foreign" domain, and because they involved
activity within a predominantly male milieu, they were categorized
as unfit for decent Muslim girls to pursue, even for those with
the requisite standard of education. This explains why the increased potential Muslim female labor supply from secondary schools
and the universities has not decreased the female scarcity in
clerical and white-collar occupations.

Morocco substantiates this observation. It is one of the
few countries to classify the labor force by sex, religion, and
nationality. In that country the percentage *female* among all
clerical workers is surprisingly high (28.8). However, although
95 percent of the Moroccan female population is Muslim, they form
only 3.5 percent of the total clerical group and 13.1 percent of
women clerical workers. An additional 14 percent are Israeli
Moroccans, and the balance are all foreign nationals.

Recent political events in the Middle East have made white-
collar employment more accessible to Muslim women. As a result
of the departure of many foreigners and members of the religious
minorities following the war crisis of 1956, substantial openings
have accrued in clerical positions. The nationalization of commercial and industrial establishments also has meant that Arabic,
rather than foreign, education is a prerequisite for employment
(except in Pakistan). It will be interesting to see if in the
next decade these new opportunities will outweigh the social
stigmata attached to this particular occupation.

Middle Eastern sex-segregation is not as evident at the
professional level as it is in clerical employment. University-
trained women show a very high propensity to work and an almost
exclusive emphasis upon professional employment. As indicated
earlier, women furnish four times as many workers to the professions as they do to the labor force as a whole in Syria; three
times as many in Egypt, and twice as many in Turkey and Libya.
In Morocco, once again, there is a wide discrepancy between the

---

National Bank, less than 30 percent were Muslims; of the 263 in
Shell Company, the percent of Muslim women was only 5.3
[Woodsmall, 1956:33; International Labor Review, 1953:316;
Lacouture, 1958:407].

female ratio in the professions, in general, and the proportion of Muslim females. Thus, although 14 percent of the
Moroccan professional workers are female, only a third of them
are *Muslim* women.

The lower representation of Middle Eastern than of Latin
American women in the professions is partly explained by their
more recent access to university-level education. However, the
possibility must not be overlooked that the number of women in
the Middle Eastern professional work force is also influenced by
their restricted acceptance into the professional ranks.

For the educated Middle Eastern woman, almost exclusively
confined as she is to teaching and nursing, teaching continues to
be the most sought after career because it offers her employment
opportunities and social acceptance. Nursing is less attractive
because opportunities are limited to gynecology and pediatrics.
Middle Easterners may rationalize their preference for the teaching profession as a female pursuit on the grounds that "it com-
bines occupational emancipation with roles traditionally ascribed
to women" [Forget, 1962:105; Woodsmall, 1956:32]. It is more
likely that this acceptance is due in large part to the conservative and secluded atmosphere the teaching profession provides.
Sex segregation at all postprimary levels in public and private
schools has naturally feminized the teaching profession in all
preparatory, secondary, and vocational girls' schools. Under
such circumstances, a woman is guaranteed a professional career
in the exclusive company of her own sex. This unique and insular
situation afforded by the teaching profession may well be responsible for the general resistance in Middle Eastern society to
redefine what jobs outside of teaching are appropriate or acceptable for educated and respectable girls to pursue.

Chapter 4

FEMALE LABOR SUPPLY AND EDUCATIONAL ACHIEVEMENT

The dissimilarity in female employment rates between Latin America and the Middle East cannot be explained away by regional differences in either the level of economic development or the structure of demand in the labor market. The negative influence of these two economic variables suggests that the regional discrepancy may stem from conditions which control the supply of women available to the labor market.

The task now is to single out the influence of conditioning factors and to test their relative importance to regional differentials in female employment rates. This chapter, then, focuses on the level of female education in both regions with the purpose of assessing whether substantial differences *do* exist in women's achievement in the educational sphere, and if they do, what influence they exert upon women's propensity to seek and obtain employment.

As the quest begins, with a concern for female education per se, certain pertinent questions compel attention. What is the extent and scope of female education in the countries under study? How does it differ from that offered to men? How functional is female instruction in both societies in preparing women for employment opportunities? The statistical relationship between women's educational achievements and the female nonagricultural employment rates in the two regions are dealt with later.

Female Education in Latin America and the Middle East

In societies where general illiteracy is high and female illiteracy even higher, female education is held to be "the single most sensitive measure of socioeconomic status and modernization . . . reflecting attitudes relating to the education of females and capacities to finance education which, for females, is still viewed by many as a luxury" [Lughod, 1965:252]. The cogency of female education, then, transcends the basic acquisition of knowledge and skills required by the nonagricultural labor force. It also carries strong connotations of a woman's social and economic position. Education is a necessary condition for a woman's participation in economic life as well as in cultural and political activities. As such, the extent to which educational opportunities are made available to women reflects the attitudes of society toward alternatives and activities deemed legitimate for the female population to pursue outside the traditional roles of marriage and childbearing.

In comparing the educational status of women in Latin America and the Middle East, three types of educational measures are available for examination: the literacy rates; the current distribution of population in urban areas by educational status; and the enrollment ratios in secondary and higher education. The literacy rates give some quantitative indication of the differences in educational level between populations and, when separated by age groups, reflect time changes. Nonetheless, they fail to describe the quality of education among the literate group. The other two measures are more qualitative. The current distribution of the total and urban population by specific educational level indicates the quality of human resources available for employment in the nonagricultural sector. The female enrollment ratios in secondary and in higher education denote trends within each society for educating the present generation of adolescents.

Illiteracy Levels.--Mere figures on the percentage of the population able to read and write long ago lost their significance for currently industrialized societies where the majority of the population has far more than these elementary skills. Throughout much of the developing world, however, the proportion of literacy is still the best available indicator of educational level [Smith, 1955:249].

In general, Latin American and Middle Eastern countries show sharp differences in educational status of their populations. Table 11 delineates vividly the illiteracy differentials between the urban and general population, between males and females, and between Latin America and the Middle East. In Latin America the percentage of illiteracy within the total population ranges from 14 to 40, with a mean of 25.9 percent. In the Middle East the corresponding range of variation is from 50 to 86 percent, with a mean of 69.9. The most literate Middle Eastern country, Turkey, has a higher rate of illiteracy (49.6 percent) than the least literate Latin American country, Peru (39.9 percent).

Equally striking in this regional comparison is that sex differentials in literacy levels also differ widely. In developing countries, in general, it is reasonable to expect an unequal distribution of illiteracy between the sexes, but in the Middle East the gap is particularly pronounced: 56 percent of the men but 83 percent of the women are illiterate. In Latin America the corresponding ratios are 22 percent for men and 29 percent for women.

43

TABLE 11

GENERAL POPULATION AND URBAN SECTOR ILLITERACY RATES,
LATIN AMERICA AND MIDDLE EAST

| | Percent Illiteracy | | | | |
| | General Population | | | Urban Sector | |
	Total	Male	Female	Male	Female
Latin America					
Chile	16.0	16.8	17.1	7.8	11.4
Colombia	26.0	25.4	27.8	n.a.	n.a.
Costa Rica	14.3	14.1	15.2	4.0	6.8
Mexico	33.0	30.3	35.5	9.6	23.7
Peru	39.9	26.2	52.4	9.5	26.8
Average	25.9	22.5	29.6	7.7	17.2
Middle East					
Egypt	70.8	57.2	84.2	39.3	68.6
Iran	69.6	58.4	81.6	36.9	61.3
Libya	73.3	56.8	90.9	n.a.	n.a.
Morocco	86.2	78.1	94.0	n.a.	n.a.
Syria	65.0	46.5	83.2	29.8	63.6
Turkey	49.6	32.5	67.3	17.0	44.9
Average	69.0	54.9	83.5	30.7	59.6

Sources: Chile, 1964:Table 6; Colombia, 1967:Table 21;
Costa Rica, 1966:Table 72; Mexico, 1962:Table 19;
Peru, 1964:Table 8; Egypt, 1963:Table 6; Iran, 1968:
Table 6; Libya, 1966:Tables 18, 19; Syria, 1962:
Table 6; Turkey, 1969:Table 26; UN, 1964:Table 13;
UN, 1965:Table 33; UNESCO, 1966:Table 4.

The effect of the large Middle Eastern sex differential has been to widen the gap in literacy standards between the two regions, especially as it relates to women. Whereas in Latin America less than one-third of the women are unable to read and write, in the Middle East more than four-fifths are similarly handicapped. Even when countries such as Chile and Costa Rica are excluded from the Latin American count because their literacy levels are atypically high for that region, the interregional differential in female illiteracy is still considerable.

When urban/rural residence is introduced as a control, the literacy rates invariably increase. The strength of the urban variable reduces illiteracy in the Middle East from almost 55 to slightly more than 30 percent for males and from 83 to 60 percent for females. Contrast this with urban Latin America, where, on the average, roughly 8 percent of all males and 17 percent of all females are unable to read and write.

One other way to underline the regional differences in female literacy levels is by examining the age-specific illiteracy rates by country. This is done in Table 12. As can be seen, female literacy rates generally differ by age, but the contrast is sharper in the Latin American countries between women aged 40 and over and those within the 15 to 39 ranges. In the Middle East, however, the hard crust of illiteracy is breaking more slowly. The percentage of women who are literate increases only slightly among the younger age groups. In Iran and Libya, in fact, the chance for a woman who is now between 25 and 29 years of age to be illiterate is almost as high as it was thirty years ago.

A glance at the age-specific illiteracy rates of females within the 15 to 19 age group provides substantial evidence to support the view that in the Middle East the grip of tradition is very tight and not as amenable to relaxation as might have been expected. For example, among every 100 girls between 15 and 19, an average of 67 are still unable to read and write. Contrast this with the Latin American countries, where the corresponding proportion is 17 percent, a 50 percent differential. Urban Middle Eastern women show considerably higher literacy although in no way parallel to that of Latin America. Among the same 15 to 19 age group, an average of 32 percent of urban women are still illiterate, compared to only 9 percent of Latin American urban women.

Urban Population Distribution and Educational Status.-- The foregoing discussion has established marked differences in the literacy levels between Latin America and the Middle East and has shown that there is a strong tendency to minimize educational opportunities for women in the Middle East. Not much has been said, however, regarding the applicability of women's

TABLE 12

AGE-SPECIFIC ILLITERACY RATES OF FEMALE POPULATIONS:
LATIN AMERICA AND THE MIDDLE EAST

Age	Latin America					Middle East				
	Colombia	Costa Rica		Mexico		Iran		Libya	Turkey	
	Total	Total	Urban	Total	Urban	Total	Urban	Total	Total	Urban
10+	27.8	15.3	6.8	35.5	23.7	81.6	61.3	95.7	67.3	44.9
10–14	23.1	7.9	2.7	28.4	15.6	62.1	23.6	---	42.6	17.4
15–19	16.1	8.2	2.7	27.2	14.9	70.7	40.6	84.3	48.4	22.3
20–24	20.5	12.1	4.2	31.5	18.8	79.7	56.7	93.3	59.5	34.3
25–29	24.3	16.3	5.8	35.8	21.4	86.2	68.1	97.0	69.9	45.4
30–34	27.2	18.7	7.5	30.0	24.6	89.6	75.1	98.1	76.4	51.8
35–39	31.2					89.7	75.2	98.4		
40–44	34.0	22.9	12.7	44.9	29.4	90.9	79.3	99.4	85.1	62.9
45–49	36.4					90.9	80.0			
50–54	41.3	33.0	20.6	52.3	36.7	93.3	85.5	99.2	91.7	76.6
55–59	40.1					94.0	85.7			
60–64	49.6	33.0	20.6	57.7	43.5	95.0	92.1	99.6	94.6	84.9
65+	55.6	---	---			95.3	90.0	99.8		

Sources: Derived from sources listed on Table 11.

educational preparation to nonagricultural labor force require-
ments. In this section and the next, the educational statistics
presented are directed specifically toward their adequacy in
preparing women for nonagricultural employment. It is the differences in employment behavior among women within the potential
range of the working ages that have to be explained.

Table 13 presents census data regarding the distribution
of the female population in four countries by specific educational
levels for the total country and for the urban areas. The information reported includes women who have completed or who have
attended some years of schooling at each stage of education. Unfortunately, not all of the countries under study provide adequate
data from which to compute the educational distribution. Nevertheless, the available information permits a fair comparison to
be drawn between feminine educational standards in two Latin
American and two Middle Eastern countries. This is felt to be
more substantive than a mere regional contrast in illiteracy
levels.

The following general trends can be extrapolated from
Table 13. In Latin America four women in five, on average, are
"literate." The proportion of literates is boosted by the considerably larger percentage of women who attend than who complete
elementary grade schools. In Chile and Costa Rica, for example,
between three-fifths and three-fourths of all females aged ten
and older are reported at the primary level. However, only 17
percent actually complete their primary education; 11 percent
continue to secondary schools; and 3 percent pursue a higher
education. Latin American countries, on the whole, report a
high rate of dropouts. In Chile, between 1959 and 1960, only
28.6 percent of the school-age population completed primary
education. In 1960 only 20 percent of a given age cohort which
had started its primary education in 1954 entered the secondary
school level [Blitz, 1964:306].

In Latin America the urban-rural differences in female
education are quite pronounced, as evidenced by the differential
between the educational standards of the total population relative
to that of the urban areas. Twice as many urban women are literate; twice as many have benefited from higher training institutes
or the university. Stated in other terms, among every 100 urban
women, more than 90 are literate; 21 have been exposed to or have
completed secondary schooling; and 5 have received training at
higher educational levels.

In the Middle East, among every 100 women in the total
population, only 20 are "literate"; 12 have attended (but less
than 11 have completed) the elementary grades; only 2 of all
those aged ten and older have continued or completed secondary

TABLE 13

DISTRIBUTION BY EDUCATIONAL LEVELS OF TOTAL AND URBAN FEMALE POPULATION:
CHILE, COSTA RICA, EGYPT, AND TURKEY

| Educational Levels | Latin America | | | | Middle East | | | |
| | Chile | | Costa Rica | | Egypt | | Turkey[a] | |
	Total	Urban	Total	Urban	Total	Urban	Total	Urban
Population Totals[b]	2,722,327	1,744,825	437,764	176,708	8,948,537	3,296,697	10,418,948	3,784,590
Percent Distribution								
Illiterate	17.1	10.7	15.2	6.8	84.2	68.5	67.3	44.9
Primary	59.0	60.1	73.3	70.5	13.3	25.0	19.4	32.0
Secondary	18.0	23.7	9.2	20.9	2.3	5.8	1.9	5.9
Higher Education	3.7	4.9	2.1	4.5	0.2	0.7	1.7	5.4
Unknown	2.2	0.6	0.2	---	---	---	9.7	11.8

[a]Refers to population who actually completed education at each educational level.
[b]Figures for females aged 10+ except for Turkey, which is 11+.

Sources: Chile, 1964:Table 2.3.2; Costa Rica, 1966:Tables 65, 72; Egypt, 1963:Table 6; Turkey, 1969: Tables 28, 29.

48

school training, and one-half of one has been exposed to or has completed higher educational levels, including the university.

The urban figures mark a slight improvement. Illiteracy levels are still high (approximately six women in ten are illiterate). However, the percentage of urban women who have attended primary education, secondary schooling, and higher educational levels is three times higher than it is in the total population.

The comparative differences in feminine education between Latin American and Middle Eastern countries can now be enumerated. In Latin America there are typically four times as many literate women as there are in the Middle East, six times as many with primary schooling, six times as many with secondary schooling, and five times as many who have benefited from education at higher institutions, including the university.

With respect to the urban population, in both Chile and Costa Rica 91 percent of all urban women are literate, compared to only 42 percent in Egypt and Turkey. These two Latin American countries can boast of more than twice as many urban women with primary schooling and more than three times as many with secondary schooling as urban female populations in the Middle East. At the higher levels of education, the regional differential shrinks considerably; only twice as many women in urban Chile and Costa Rica benefit from higher training, compared to their urban counterparts in the Middle East.

Female Enrollment in Secondary and Higher Education

The third education measure to be discussed pertains to women's enrollment at the second and third levels of education. In constructing Table 14 an attempt was made to have the data on female enrollment correspond as closely as possible to the specific year for which female labor force statistics were compiled. Table 14 deals with the number of women enrolled at the second level of education—including general secondary (academic) schools, vocational training, and teacher-training institutes—and at higher institutions including the university.

It may be conceivable that in some of the developing countries under study secondary and vocational schools have become accessible to the nonurban populations, but it is legitimate to assume that, on the whole, higher education is available only in the urban context. Consequently, female enrollment ratios at higher levels of education have been computed with the urban population only as base. A second assumption is that ages 15 to 19 are typical years for secondary school enrollment and ages 20 to 24 for enrollment at higher institutions and

49

TABLE 14

FEMALE ENROLLMENT AT SECONDARY AND HIGHER LEVELS OF EDUCATION
(c.1960)

Region and Country	Secondary Level, Aged 15 to 19			Higher Levels, Aged 20 to 24	
	Women as Percent of All Enrollees	Ratio Enrolled/ All Women — Total Population	Ratio Enrolled/ All Women — Urban Population	Women as Percent of All Enrollees	Ratio Enrolled/ All Women
Latin America					
Chile	50.0	30.7	42.4	35.0	3.9
Colombia	42.0	16.6	27.5	23.0	2.3
Costa Rica	50.0	15.4	38.3	42.0	14.3
Ecuador	45.0	23.9	59.0	23.0	4.8
Mexico	48.0	7.4	14.0	17.0	2.8
Peru	27.0	32.3	62.2	26.0	3.8
Average	43.6	21.0	40.5	27.6	5.3
Middle East					
Egypt	27.0	14.2	34.3	17.0	5.0
Iran	31.0	19.1	44.6	24.0	2.8
Morocco	26.0	6.2	17.0	14.0	0.4
Pakistan	16.0	6.6	---	12.0	3.7
Syria	22.0	11.4	27.5	17.0	7.9
Turkey	28.0	14.0	68.0	21.0	6.8
Average	24.9	11.9	32.4	17.5	4.4

Sources: Urban population [UN, 1965:Table 27]; except for Costa
Rica [1966:Table 48]; Colombia [1967:Table 7];
Ecuador [1964:Table 1]; Mexico [1962:Table 8]; Egypt
[1963:Table 2]; Iran [1968:Table 1]. Enrollment
figures [UNESCO, 1970:Tables 2.9 and 2.12].

universities.[1] The ratios thus obtained are only approximations
and are not fully reliable for comparative purposes because of
the uncertainties in regard to the actual age composition of
students at the two levels. These limitations are borne in mind
when the comparative regional differences are discussed.

Latin American girls, except in Peru, comprise close to
50 percent of the total enrollment at second levels of education.
Among the 15 to 19 age group, two girls in every ten in the
general population and four in every ten in the urban population
attend secondary/vocational schools. The enrollment ratios are
highest in Peru, Ecuador, and Chile and lowest in Mexico and
Colombia.

In the Middle East, typically, almost one-fourth of the
students attending secondary or vocational schools are female.
In Iran and Turkey the female proportion rises to one-third.
The enrollment ratios show that between the ages of 15 and 19
one in ten girls in the total population and one in three in the
urban population is enrolled at a secondary or vocational school.
The chance for a girl in this age range to attend secondary
schools is highest in Egypt, Iran, and Turkey, lowest in Libya,
Morocco, and Pakistan.

The comparative regional differences in enrollment ratios
for the 15 to 19 age group indicate that among the total population the proportion of women enrolled is twice as large in the
Latin American countries as it is in the Middle East. When urban
residence is introduced as a control for this age group, however,
the disparity is reduced to four in ten for Latin America versus
three in ten for the Middle East.

The interregional differential is minimal when we compare
the proportions of Latin American and Middle Eastern women in
the 20 to 24 year age range who are enrolled in higher education.
Table 14 shows that within this age range one in twenty Latin
American women is enrolled and one in twenty-five Middle Eastern
women. The regional difference appears in the *proportion* of
women in the total student body. Of all enrollment in higher
education, Latin American women constitute close to 28 percent,
Middle Eastern women only 18 percent.

How Functional is Female Education in the Two Regions?

So far it has been shown that differences in female
educational achievement are pronounced at every level. Among

---

[1]This procedure is followed by Harbison and Myers [1964:29-
30].

the total population, the Latin American countries can generally
count on six times as many women with primary, with secondary,
and with higher educational training as can those in the Middle
East. Again this differential is reduced considerably in the
urban areas, particularly for higher education. Furthermore,
and counter to possible initial expectations, it is evident from
Table 14 that the enrollment ratios of Middle Eastern women
currently aged 15 to 24 do not lag far behind those of Latin
America. The interregional gap in urban female secondary school
enrollment is reduced considerably; it virtually disappears at
higher education and university levels.

Before we examine the relationship that exists between
these educational differences and the regional disparity in female employment rates, one other aspect of education must be
discussed--the adequacy of curricula in preparing women for occupational participation.

In most developing nations the only institutionalized
mode of social and economic ascent in recent years has been
through professional employment. This factor has laid heavy
emphasis upon professional education and upon "a strong university
orientation." Generally in most developing countries, most people
cannot pursue their education because of obvious and valid economic reasons. The typical situation exhibits two extremes--
an enormous number of illiterates unevenly counterbalanced by
a proportionately sizable number of highly educated persons. The
imbalance between the underprivileged, who remain illiterate,
and the economically able, who strive for professional education,
is particularly acute among males but has not left females un-
affected. To illustrate, consider the situation in Egypt in
1960 when 70 percent of the population aged ten and older was
illiterate. Yet Egypt at that time, and in proportion to the
total population, turned out an annual quota of university
graduates as high as or even higher than Great Britain or the
Scandinavian countries despite immense differences in the general
literacy and educational levels. Another educational paradox:
Egypt is the only Arab country that can meet the growing need
for teachers not only at home but also in all other Middle Eastern
countries [Heller, 1963:167].

The repercussions of a strong university orientation
upon the educational system are felt at two levels: (1) the
secondary school curricula tend to be designed almost exclusively
along "academic" lines; (2) the emphasis on professional employment is so strong among the educated that a university graduate
feels compelled to refuse any occupation not carrying professional
prestige. No attempt is made to diversify teaching by developing
programs for those unwilling or unable to continue further academic training. This means that a person with a secondary

certificate is virtually unequipped and unprepared to fill a
middle-level position.

Both these factors, in varying degrees, have been influential in both regions. Latin American countries, however,
appear to have been more successful than Middle Eastern in over-
coming the educational imbalance by mobilizing the school system
for the purpose of specific vocational training.[2] A glance at
the secondary school enrollment statistics classified by specific
areas of emphasis indicates that in Latin America there is a
greater tendency for the diversification of secondary school programs. In those societies, among every 100 female secondary school
students, roughly 60 are in the general (academic) program, 30
in vocational training, and 8 in teacher-training institutes.
In the Middle East, by contrast, 80 percent of all female secondary school students pursue the academic line; 15 percent are in
vocational training; and 5 percent in teacher training.

In countries such as Iran, Pakistan, and Syria, although
the student body in vocational training schools is almost exclusively male, there are a number of women enrolled in domestic
science vocational institutions who represent an almost total
loss to the potential labor force. An Egyptian follow-up on
these women showed that 70 percent married immediately upon com-
pleting their three- to four-year training course. This "loss"
does not seem to bother official educators who hold that "there
is no waste in spending time and money in preparing women to
become good housewives" [Boktor, 1963:66].

The reasons for the reluctance of Middle Eastern women
to attend vocational schools and other *nonacademic* training institutions are legitimate. First, the governments in most Middle
Eastern nations have contented themselves with establishing
numerous intermediate-level schools without attempting to change
the overall structure and occupational opportunity within the
exchange sector. Second, despite the many patriotic appeals to
women in Middle Eastern countries to participate in the "national
struggle to reconstruct the fatherland," no genuine steps have
been taken at any social level toward redefining what types of
jobs other than teaching are appropriate or socially acceptable
for an educated and respectable Muslim girl to pursue.

Two excellent examples of these incongruencies are the
nursing profession and the clerical occupations. Nursing,
equated with domestic service, is reserved for the lower classes.

---

[2]For an excellent discussion challenging the view that more
vocational schooling is needed in developing countries, refer
to Foster [1964:140].

As for clerical occupations, it was shown earlier that in all
Middle Eastern countries the clerical and administrative ladder
from the bottom up is manned with male workers and that until
very recently, almost all female secretaries, receptionists,
salesgirls, and bank tellers were non-Muslims. Recent political
events in the Middle East may pave the way for acceptance of female white-collar employment as an alternative to the professions.
As yet, it is still considered degrading for a university-graduate
Middle Eastern woman to be employed in a clerical position.

Unless the pay and status of intermediate occupations
are raised it is doubtful whether vocational schools in the
Middle East will be associated with anything higher than manual
labor; hence with lower class involvement [Futuh, 1951:173-183].
A girl from the middle strata is obviously not going to attend
such schools, whereas a girl from lower income groups may think
twice about it. As expectation goals, jobs in these categories
offer little incentive. They carry the same low prestige and
same low pay as domestic work which requires none of the academic
training yet offers many compensations in kind (such as clothing,
vacation trips, medical expenses, and the like) which do not
accrue under formal employment conditions.

One other area in which the Latin American education system has proved to be more successful than the Middle Eastern is
in the content of the curricula promulgated in the academic program. In most Latin American countries the secondary-school
curricula include as an integral part of their program courses
in typing, bookkeeping, accounting, and so on, all of which
equip the bulk of secondary students who opt to discontinue academic training with definite intermediate skills. Such facilities
are not provided in the Middle East.

Female Education and Labor Supply

Having identified some of the major comparative differences in female educational standards between the Latin American
and Middle Eastern countries, the next immediate concern pertains
to the relationship between these educational differences and
the regional disparity in female employment rates. More specifically, the following questions are pertinent: Is education
a major condition affecting the supply of women available to the
Latin American and Middle Eastern labor markets? Are educated
women at a competitive advantage in the labor market relative
to the noneducated? Do women with higher education display a
greater propensity to employment than those with less? If so,
can part or all of the explanation for the feminine differential
in the nonagricultural employment rates be sought in the educational differences that have been shown to exist in the two
populations? And, ultimately, what difference would it have

54

made to the overall nonagricultural female employment rates if women were as educated in the Middle East as they are in Latin America?

The relationship between female labor supply and education is complex. Sending women of labor force age to school, rather than to work, is one way of decreasing the labor supply at ages where secondary and university education are still incomplete. The effect of this "loss" could be substantial since the major groups affected range between ages 15 and 24, typically the ages at which women show a high (if not the highest) propensity for gainful employment.

On the other hand, higher levels of education are known to whet the female propensity toward employment. They have invested time and money in education and desire to use it in some meaningful way. Moreover, education gives women a competitive advantage relative to men in the labor market and access to a greater abundance of attractive jobs.

Following this line of analysis, the first question that presents itself for investigation is whether female education in the countries under study has operated to decrease the supply of women at ages 15 to 24 available to the labor market. A convenient way to assess whether a loss has in fact occurred is to test the influence of female attendance at second and third levels of education upon the corresponding age-specific labor force rates. A second question of interest pertains to the actual influence of education upon women's involvement in the nonagricultural labor force. This can be derived by cross-classifying the nonagricultural female workers by educational status and then computing the percentage women workers constitute of each specific educational group.

The Effect of School Enrollment Upon Labor Force Participation.--For the purpose of this discussion it will be assumed that all women currently attending secondary and higher educational institutions are "lost" to the active job market. To examine the effect of this loss upon the labor force rates, let us hypothesize that if these women had been in the work force they would have manifested the same propensity to be employed as the rest of the female population within that age group. It is only in some of the Latin American countries, particularly Chile and to a lesser extent Peru, where female enrollment at secondary levels of education has reduced the number of the "would-be" economically active female segment between the ages of 15 and 19. On the average, the age-specific activity rates of that age group are raised by five percentage points when the number of potential additional (but "lost") workers is added to the actual number of women workers in the nonagricultural labor force. If one accepts that 113,873 Chilean women between 15 and 19 were

recently enrolled in secondary or vocational training and that
they had the same propensity to be employed in nonagricultural
activities as other girls in that age group, an additional
26,760 hypothetical female workers would be obtained. A recom-
putation of the age-specific activity rates of the 15 to 19 age
group, on a base which includes the actual and the additional
numbers of female workers, yields a seven percentage point increase
over the actual age-specific activity rates. In other words, had
those Chilean girls not been enrolled in secondary and vocational
schools, the age-specific labor force rates for the 15 to 19 age
group would have been 30.7 instead of 23.5 percentage points. In
the Middle East, however, the effect of adding the hypothetical
population of additional female workers to the number actually in
the nonagricultural labor force fails to increase the age-specific
activity rate of the 15 to 19 age group. For the region as a
whole, since the difference between the actual and the expected
age-specific labor force rate is *less than one percentage point*,
removing the very small number of women enrolled in secondary
schools makes no appreciable difference.

In both Latin America and the Middle East the number of
women enrolled in institutions of higher education is too meager
to influence the labor force activity rates of the 20 to 24 age
group. In both regions the difference between the actual and
the hypothetical activity rates of female workers in this age
group is *less than one percentage point*. Therefore the combination of all these findings leads to two conclusions: first, in
Latin America and in the Middle East female enrollment in secondary and higher education *does not affect* the supply of women to
the labor market. Second, the regional differences in female
enrollment ratios at second and third levels of education cannot
be invoked to explain the dissimilarity in female employment rates
between two regions. It still remains to be seen, however,
whether differences in educational levels among the total female
population are reflected in women's work participation rates.

Education-Specific Activity Rates

Labor force studies conducted in the United States have
shown a substantial relationship between female education and
employment [Bancroft, 1958:65-67]. The higher the level of her
education, the greater the chance of a woman's employability.
Some of the mechanisms whereby educational differences are translated into work-participation differentials are: the availability
of alternatives outside of and within marriage; the alternatives
outside of motherhood; the placement of women at a competitive
advantage to men in the labor market; women's desire to utilize
their training in some meaningful capacity.

Whether or not educational differences are translated
into work participation differentials also depends upon the labor
market and upon the extent to which economic activities are
sufficiently differentiated to offer occupational opportunities
to educated females. The information presented in Chapter III
showed the prevalence in Latin American and Middle Eastern societies of a considerable number of traditional-type occupations--
service, petty trade, handicraft, and home industry--all of which
require very little skill or training beyond the attainment of
the ordinary housewife. Evidently, then, a labor market does
exist for the noneducated female. But there is also a modern
work force in which Middle Eastern and Latin American women participate, and it is there where the influence of the educational
factor is expected to be manifest.

Table 15 indicates the education-specific labor force
rate of nonagricultural female workers in Chile, Colombia, Egypt,
Syria, and Turkey, the only countries for which information on
their educational status is available. This table shows the percentage of such women workers within each specific educational
group. In all but Colombia the urban population is taken as a
base. As can be seen, except in Chile there is a positive relationship between educational levels and nonfarm employment:
the labor force rates are accelerated at each successive level
of education. This trend is particularly marked in the Middle
Eastern countries where the tendency of education to accelerate
the female employment rates is clearly progressive: each educational increment is reflected in a corresponding increase in the
level of women's participation in the nonagricultural work force.
In Turkey, Syria, and Egypt less than 4 percent of all women with
partial or complete primary education are working, but among those
with secondary schooling 21 percent are employed. The positive
effect of education upon the employability of Middle Eastern
women is most evident at the highest educational levels. Among
the university trained an average of two women in three are in
the labor force.

Colombian work participation rates do not reflect sharply
women's incremental educational levels. Part of this blurring
is attributable to basing the computations on the total rather
than on the urban female population only, which may have depressed
the employment rates of the more highly educated women. But note,
for example, that in urban Chile 33 percent of all illiterate
women are in the nonagricultural labor force versus only 6 percent in Middle Eastern countries. This discrepancy may simply
reflect that Latin American illiterate or barely educated women
simply have greater nonfarm opportunities. In fact, their employability chances are just as high as are those for women with
partial or complete secondary schooling or with vocational and
technical training. In the Middle Eastern countries, by contrast,
the increase yielded in the education-specific labor force rates

TABLE 15

EDUCATION-SPECIFIC LABOR FORCE RATES OF NONAGRICULTURAL FEMALE
WORKERS IN URBAN AREAS: LATIN AMERICA AND THE MIDDLE EAST
(c.1960)

Level of Education	Chile[a]	Colom-bia[b]	Egypt	Syria	Turkey[c]
Illiterate	33.3	n.a.	8.9	6.5	3.0
Primary	31.8	20.6	2.9	4.3	4.3
Secondary	26.0	24.5	24.4	25.6	13.3
Technical/Vocational	30.6	n.a.	n.a.	n.a.	30.5
Higher/University	61.6	41.4	70.5	55.5	69.4

[a]Computed on basis of educational status of total female
labor force which includes 96 percent of nonagricultural female
workers.

[b]Education-specific activity rates computed on basis of
educational status of total population rather than urban only.

[c]Data on educational status of female workers refer to
educational levels *completed*.

Sources: Chile, 1964:Table 3.4.5; Colombia, 1967:Tables 21, 29;
Egypt, 1963:Tables 31, 41; Syria, 1961:Table 36;
Turkey, 1969:Tables 43, 43a.

between primary and secondary educational levels ranges from a
three-fold increase in Turkey to an eight-fold increase in Egypt
(Table 15).

Two factors suggest themselves as possible explanations
for this regional difference. The first is that in Latin America
the better educated women marry in greater proportion than the
poorly educated and have young children to care for. This would
be, however, in direct contradiction to the general findings concerning the effect of higher education upon age-at-marriage and
upon fertility rates. In Chile, for example, the average number
of live births for married women at the end of their fertile
period diminishes by at least 50 percent from one educational
extreme to the other, from 4.4 to 2.1 children per woman in the
educational continuum from no formal education to completion of
the university [Tabah, 1964:22-23]. It would be more reasonable
to assume that the better educated marry somewhat later than the
less educated, and that they are the least to suffer from the
encumbrances of early and high fertility.

The other possibility is that the nonagricultural labor
force in Latin America is mostly filled from the ranks of the
lower-income groups, hence the poorly educated. This could
imply that the labor market is highly undifferentiated and that
a very large proportion of jobs require few or no specific skills.
It is also possible that many women learn on the job. The more
work-experience there is, the more skills are acquired except
in the professions and technical services. The only data which
show the extent to which the Latin American labor market is
differentiated with competitive groups at various levels is the
occupational composition of the work force. The differentiation
by sex shows the preponderance of the less-educated women to be
in one major category: domestic service. It will be remembered
that in Latin America approximately four in ten female workers
are employed in private household work.

Unless an over-reporting of the educational status of
women workers has occurred in the Middle East, the situation
there appears to be quite different. In those societies the
accelerating effect of education upon women's employment rates
suggests that there are either more job opportunities for trained
persons (regardless of sex), or educated women are more willing
to work, or both.

The high propensity for the well-educated woman to work
is facilitated by the inverse relationships education holds to
fertility and marriage. Survey results in Egypt show that for
each 100 wives, those with a university education have 394 children; with secondary education, 583; with primary-elementary,
703; and with illiteracy, 708. Put another way, for every
100 children born to illiterate Egyptian women, 87 are born to

women who read and write, 63 to women with secondary certificates, and 53 to women with university degrees [El Badry, 1956:22-34].

A cross-classification by education and marital status shows that highest illiteracy rates are reported among married women and lowest among single women. In addition, more than 50 percent of all adult Egyptian Muslim females who have completed their secondary or university education are single, whereas in the total adult Muslim population only 12 percent are single. It is, of course, possible that the higher educated women who are actually working are from the non-Muslim groups. This is difficult to verify, however, since the census does not provide a cross-classification of the labor force by religious affiliation and by education.

The high participation rates manifested by university educated women in Latin America and the Middle East indicate both the demand for professional and technical services in those societies and the positive response with which highly educated women meet this demand. In connection with women's response rate the suggestion has been made that in traditional societies the employment of university-educated women, particularly in professional capacities, does not meet the usual type of resistance and censure.

Commenting on the economic activity of married women in Puerto Rico, Carleton was struck by the fact that the distribution is just the opposite of that expected on the basis of economic need.

Instead of finding a concentration of economically active women in the lower educational levels where income is also the lowest, the distribution is skewed at the other end. Proportionately, very few women with little education are economically active. With increasing education economic activity reaches a level as high for the married woman if not higher than that of the United States [1965: 233].

Several possibilities may explain the prevalence of such attitudes. One is that in both regions female university students tend to come from elite strata, of wealth or at least of social position. By virtue of their privileged locus in the social structure these women can deviate from the norm that relegates females to the home. By the same token their fathers, brothers, and husbands can afford to accord them the role of pioneers of social change.

A second possibility is that in developing societies most of the university-educated women enter the highly prestigious ranks of the professions and often occupy important positions. This salutary shift in status serves to cure husbands of their scruples and hurt pride and enables them to fend off the charge that they cannot provide alone for their families [Carleton, 1965:235]. There are other practical factors operating in Latin American and Middle Eastern societies to encourage the educated woman to work. Typically, in those societies, the university-trained woman is well-to-do and can afford domestic help and labor-saving devices, which free her to an extent not possible for less privileged women.

The Effect of Increasing Female Educational Standards in the Middle East Upon the Labor Force Rates

Given the accelerating effect of educational levels upon the nonagricultural employment rate, what would the work participation rates in the Middle East be if women in those countries were as highly educated as their counterparts in Latin America? The question is legitimate from the supply point of view. There is no reason to assume that the further spread of education among Middle Eastern women would in any way inhibit their willingness to work.

The effect of educational differences upon female employment rates in both regions has been tested by subjecting the female population of Turkey and Egypt, first, to the educational standard of urban Chile (as an example of the most highly educated country in Latin America) and, second, to the educational standards of Colombia (as a more typical example of educational standards in the Latin American region).

The results of both standardization procedures verify the positive influence of differences in educational levels when the "expected" effects of education upon nonagricultural labor force rates are compared with the "actual" rates. Upon standardization the observed nonagricultural female employment rates of *urban* women are raised from 6.1 to 18.2 percent in Egypt and from 9.1 to 12.3 percent in Turkey. When the educational standards of the total female population are taken as base for standardization analysis, the results obtained show an increase in the overall female participation rates from 3.5 to 7.0 percent in Egypt and from 2.3 to 5.8 percent in Turkey.

The dissimilarity in female employment rates between the Latin American and Middle Eastern countries cannot be accounted for solely by educational differences. However, it is quite definite that the low standards of female education in the Middle Eastern world depress the supply of women available to the labor market.

Labor force rates, however, also depend upon demand, and here the grounds are more tenuous. If only a small percentage

of women are given education, demand for their services will be
great and they should expect a relatively high employment rate.
It does not follow that the employment rate will continue to
rise as more women become trained. It can be argued that in
Chile the high educational attainment of the population has led
to a standstill, if not a decline, in the demand for university-
trained people. In any such case of de-escalation, women are
the first to suffer, which could explain why the activity rate
of the female graduate is lower in Chile than it is in Turkey
or Egypt. Because of the acute shortage of professional workers
in all the Middle Eastern countries the market is still open for
female graduates, and hiring practices at the professional levels
are still indiscriminate of sex.

Despite the law of diminishing returns, it is expected
that in the Middle East the need for trained personnel at the
intermediate and upper levels of employment will continue to
grow steadily. The demand is expected to continue as long as
women can aid in economic production. The price paid for labor
may fall if more Middle Eastern women attain higher educational
degrees, but the need for their skills is expected to remain
positive for a considerable time to come. Realistically, it
will be some time before any of the Middle Eastern nations can
reach the educational standards of Chile. From this point of
view the standardization analysis concerning the effect of
Chile's educational standards upon the female employment rates
in the Middle Eastern world may be considered too hypothetical.
This should not, however, detract from the general finding that,
given adequate incentives, a tremendous female potential exists
in the Middle Eastern countries which can be channeled into
economically productive endeavors.

Chapter 5

FAMILY CHARACTERISTICS AND FEMALE LABOR SUPPLY

Lack of education among Middle Eastern women has emerged as an important variable operating to depress female employment participation rates. More importantly, the marked dissimilarity in female educational levels suggests considerable differences in attitude between Latin American and Middle Eastern societies regarding the extent to which each acknowledges the availability of legitimate alternatives to women outside of traditional family roles. These differences are explored in a later chapter. Here the inquiry continues into factors which control the supply of women available to the labor market, with the influence of one such condition singled out for detailed discussion. Specifically, the analysis is directed toward examining the marital and fertility characteristics of the female population in Latin America and in the Middle East to test their relative importance in explaining the regional disparity in the female employment rates.

The influence of marital status and fertility as major conditions controlling the supply of women available to the labor market has been explored in earlier studies [Grabill *et al.*, 1958: 262-264; Kiser *et al.*, 1968:220; Myrdal and Klein, 1956:61]. The general findings show that single, widowed, and divorced women are most active in the labor force, married women least active; and within the married group wives with children work less than those without. These influences of marriage and fertility upon the nonagricultural employment rates are also borne out by the analysis of the marital-specific employment rates of women in the countries under study. In the Latin American countries the propensity for divorced or separated women to work is five times as high as it is for married women; for the single woman the ratio is four times as high. In the Middle Eastern countries the corresponding proportions are eight and six times as high. In both regions, the chances for a widowed woman to be incorporated in the nonagricultural labor force are less than twice as high as they are for a married one (Table 16). With respect to marital fertility, the statistics for Chile show that 17 percent of all childless wives are in the labor force, compared to only 10 percent of the married mothers (Table 17).

63

TABLE 16

MARITAL-SPECIFIC LABOR FORCE RATES OF NONAGRICULTURAL
FEMALE WORKERS: LATIN AMERICA AND THE MIDDLE EAST
(c.1960)

Nonfarm Workers per Country	Overall Activity Rates Ages 12 to 64	Marital-Specific Rates				
		Single	Married	Consensual Unions	Widows	Divorced/ Separated
Latin America						
Chile	23.2	37.1	9.7	12.2	16.3	44.0
Costa Rica	16.5	33.1	7.5	6.5	10.6	32.6
Ecuador	14.5	33.9	19.6	n.a.	<——14.2——>	
Peru	15.0	29.4	7.7	7.5	11.1	55.9
Middle East						
Egypt	3.1	9.8	1.4	---	3.5	10.4
Turkey	2.3	6.5	1.4	---	1.8	15.2
Syria	2.8	8.6	1.5	---	2.2	8.5

Sources: Chile, 1964:Tables 18, 20; Costa Rica, 1966:Tables 37,
63; Ecuador, 1964:Tables 6, 9; Peru, 1964:Tables 101,
102; Egypt, 1963:Tables 8, 20, 34; Turkey, 1965:
Tables 24, 44; Syria, 1962:Table 42; UN, 1969:Table 7.

TABLE 17

ACTIVITY RATES OF TOTAL CHILEAN WOMEN BY MARITAL GROUP
AND BY FERTILITY STATUS, 1960
(Population 12+)

Marital Status	Total Number	Economically Active	Percent Active
Single			
Total	1,135,001	336,919	29.6
With children	111,323	48,722	44.0
Without children	1,024,678	288,197	28.1
Married and Consensual Unions			
Total	1,202,064	128,852	10.7
With children	994,870	94,552	9.7
Without children	207,194	34,300	17.2
Widows/Separated			
Total	277,768	68,947	24.8
With children	218,911	54,027	24.6
Without children	58,857	14,920	25.3

Source: Chile, 1964:Vols. 1-25; Statistics by Province:Tables 9-9D.

As a result of these findings studies on female employment tend to be guided by the supposition of a universal and substantial relationship between the marital and fertility characteristics of the female population and women's work-participation rates. This has bred a commonplace impression that a family system marked by such factors as late-age-at-marriage, a high degree of nonmarriage, a high incidence of marital disruption, and a low fertility schedule is conducive to large-scale involvement of women in economic activities outside the home. If this assumption is correct the presence or absence of any one of these family characteristics could influence considerably the female participation rates in any one country. It follows then, that a possible source for the striking divergency in female employment rates between Latin America and the Middle East springs from differences in marital and fertility characteristics between the two populations.

In evaluating the validity of this assumption, two lines of analysis are pursued. First, census data from the Latin American and Middle Eastern countries are examined to determine if the two populations are characterized by marked differences with respect to family characteristics assumed to be intimately related to women's employment rates. The second line of analysis is directed at testing through standardization procedures whether such differences have a positive bearing upon the female employment rates. Three family variables are discussed and analyzed: the marital status structure, the marital fertility patterns, and the age-distribution of the female population within each specific marital group.

The measure of women's work participation to be used throughout the discussion is the percentage of females within the working ages, taken to be 15 to 64, who are engaged in economic activities outside of agriculture and/or who are in the urban work force. Detailed data on the overall female employment rates and on specific rates within each age group are shown in Table 18 for each one of the countries under study, except for Mexico. In the particular case of Chile it was not possible to obtain data related to family characteristics for the nonagricultural female labor force. Likewise, much of the data on urban female workers is not cross-classified by marital and fertility characteristics. Given that Chilean women agricultural workers constitute only four percent of the total labor force, for the purpose of this analysis the whole of the female labor force in Chile will be considered as nonagricultural.

Marital Status Structure

A regional comparison of family characteristics shows that Middle Eastern countries rate very unfavorably on the availability of women to the labor market. This is due to the

66

TABLE 18

AGE-SPECIFIC ACTIVITY RATES OF NONAGRICULTURAL AND URBAN
FEMALE WORKERS: LATIN AMERICA AND THE MIDDLE EAST
(c.1960)

Country	Total Aged 15-64	Age Groups									
		15-19	20-24	25-29	30-34	35-39	40-44	45-49	50-54	55-59	60-64

Latin America

Country	Total Aged 15-64	15-19	20-24	25-29	30-34	35-39	40-44	45-49	50-54	55-59	60-64
Colombia											
Urban	17.2	19.4	← 23.2 →		← 17.3 →				← 13.5 →		
Chile											
Nonfarm	23.2	23.5	32.4	27.9	23.8	22.5	22.2	21.3	19.4	16.8	13.7
Urban	28.3	27.8	39.4	34.2	28.6	27.5	30.6	25.7	22.9	19.4	15.1
Ecuador											
Nonfarm	14.5	← 17.2 →		← 14.9 →		← 13.3 →		← 12.5 →		← 12.3 →	
Urban	28.3	← 32.5 →		← 28.4 →		← 24.5 →		← 22.7 →		← 21.2 →	
Peru											
Nonfarm	15.0	17.2	19.6	16.3	15.0	13.7	13.2	12.6	11.8	10.6	8.8
Urban	26.9	30.5	35.8	29.6	26.5	25.4	24.7	23.9	22.6	20.5	17.9
Costa Rica											
Nonfarm	16.5	17.8	23.0	19.4	17.1	17.1	15.7	14.0	11.8	9.9	8.1

Middle East

Country	Total Aged 15-64	15-19	20-24	25-29	30-34	35-39	40-44	45-49	50-54	55-59	60-64
Syria											
Nonfarm	2.3	3.5	3.5	3.4	3.0	2.6	2.4	2.2	1.9	1.8	1.2
Pakistan											
Nonfarm	2.2	1.4	1.8	← 2.1 →		← 2.7 →		← 2.8 →		← 2.5 →	
Turkey											
Nonfarm	2.3	2.7	3.7	2.4	2.1	2.7	2.7	2.7	2.6	1.8	1.5
Urban	9.1	10.4	12.4	9.6	8.7	10.3	10.9	10.3	8.2	6.5	4.6
Egypt											
Nonfarm	3.1	4.4	5.0	3.0	2.5	2.4	2.9	2.5	2.8	2.1	1.9
Iran											
Nonfarm	8.5	10.5	10.3	9.0	8.4	8.4	8.7	8.4	7.9	6.2	5.6
Urban	9.3	8.5	12.4	10.0	9.0	9.4	10.5	10.2	10.9	8.1	4.4
Libya											
Nonfarm	3.0	2.8	3.4	3.0	3.2	3.3	3.7	3.7	3.7	2.5	2.5
Morocco											
Nonfarm	5.7	5.5	5.2	← 4.9 →		← 6.4 →		← 7.2 →		← 6.3 →	
Urban	10.1	← 9.5 →		←——— 10.3 ———→			←——— 11.7 ———→				

Sources: Colombia, 1967:Tables 11, 26, 36; Chile, 1964:Tables 6, 29, 32;
Ecuador, 1964:Tables 4, 6, 8A; Peru, 1964:Tables 15, 91; Costa Rica,
1966:Tables 10, 48; Syria, 1962:Tables 27, 34; Turkey, 1969:Table 42;
Iran, 1968:Tables 1, 21; Libya, 1966:Tables 2, 49, 51; Morocco, 1960:
Tables 6, 8; UN, 1964:Table 9; UN, 1968:Table 2A.

universality of marriage in those societies, the young age-at-marriage, and the high fertility schedule among the married, all of which demonstrably depress the employability of women.

The latest census information for nine Middle Eastern countries, shown in Table 19, indicates that on the average, 90 percent of all adult women have been married, including those currently married, divorced, and widowed. Among this segment, an average of 72 percent report intact marital unions. The remainder have not remarried.

Typically, in the Middle East, only one adult woman in ten is single. Syria, Tunisia, and Turkey report the highest number of females who have never married (14 per 100), but in countries such as Libya, Morocco, and Pakistan, only *five adult women among every 100* do not marry.

Moreover, in the Middle East marriage is not only universal, but it also occurs very early in a woman's life. In Table 20 the percentage of women in the population who are single at various ages is used as an indicator of the age-at-marriage. As can be seen, in the Middle Eastern countries, over 50 percent of all females within ages 15 to 19, and 88 percent within ages 20 to 24 have already married. By age 29 there are hardly any single women left in the population. Less than five women in every 100 reach age 30 without procuring a husband. Even in countries where women tend to marry relatively later, such as Egypt and Turkey, the universality of marriage prevails. Typically, for the Middle East as a whole, the chance of finding a single woman among the population aged 35 and above is only one in a hundred.

In Latin America, by contrast, the prominence of *marital delay* and *nonmarriage* are expected to be conducive to a large-scale involvement of women in the work force. According to the latest statistics available for eight Latin American countries, an average of 57 adult women among every 100 have been married; of these, 46 percent report intact marital unions, 9 percent are widowed, and 2.4 percent are either divorced or separated from their husbands. Of the remaining 43 percent among the adult female population who have never married, 10 percent live in irregular nonlegal unions and 33 percent are single (Table 19).

It is important to point out that Latin American census data underestimate the actual frequency of nonlegalized living arrangements. For example, many women listed as single are in fact living in a consensual union, but are unwilling to admit it. More important, the entry for single women does not take into account nonlegal living arrangements that have been terminated. Once a consensual relationship is dissolved, the women enters the statistics officially as single, even when she has children.

TABLE 19

FEMALE POPULATION BY MARITAL STATUS:
LATIN AMERICA AND THE MIDDLE EAST

Region/ Country	Year	Total Women 15+	Percent Distribution by Marital Status					
			Single	Consensual Union	Legally Married	Widowed	Separated/ Divorced	Status Unknown
Latin America								
Argentina	1960	6,936,304	30.1	4.4	55.7	8.7	0.8	0.4
Chile	1960	2,306,909	35.9	3.3	48.7	9.6	2.4	---
Colombia	1964	4,843,600	37.3	9.6	43.1	8.1	1.9	---
Ecuador	1962	1,250,963	31.6	14.1	45.8	8.1	0.6	---
Mexico	1960	10,287,908	29.3	9.4	48.1	9.7	0.8	2.9
Peru	1961	2,862,352	32.5	14.2	43.3	8.9	0.5	0.8
Uruguay	1963	938,500	29.0	4.5	53.9	10.5	1.9	0.2
Venezuela	1961	2,051,650	37.3	20.1	33.6	6.7	10.0	1.2
Average			32.9	9.9	46.5	8.7	2.4	0.6
Middle East								
Algeria	1966	3,228,600	11.7	---[a]	67.0	15.0	2.9	0.5
Egypt	1960	7,252,050	12.0	---	67.6	17.3	2.0	1.1
Iran	1966	6,566,191	11.5	---	73.9	13.1	1.1	0.4
Libya	1964	369,708	4.1	---	77.3	14.1	3.8	0.7
Morocco	1960	3,299,018	7.5	---	70.1	16.0	4.2	1.4
Pakistan	1961	23,499,769	5.7	---	76.4	17.2	0.6	---
Syria	1960	1,137,460	14.3	---	71.2	12.8	0.8	0.7
Tunisia	1966	1,203,125	14.7	---	71.4	12.2	1.5	0.1
Turkey	1965	9,072,782	14.5	---	72.7	11.7	0.9	0.1
Average			10.5		72.0	14.4	1.8	0.5

[a]Consensual unions are not recognized in the Middle East.

Sources: UN, 1969:Table 7, except for Turkey [1969:Table 24].

TABLE 20

PERCENTAGES OF NEVER-MARRIED WOMEN AT VARIOUS AGES:
LATIN AMERICA AND THE MIDDLE EAST
(c.1960)

Country	Total Aged 15+ (000s)	Age Groups									
		15-19	20-24	25-29	30-34	35-39	40-44	45-49	50-54	55-59	60-64
Latin America											
Colombia	4,843	84.2	46.6	27.8	21.2	18.7	18.5	18.7	19.8	19.8	21.3
Chile	2,306	90.4	57.1	32.4	21.1	17.1	15.1	14.3	15.8	15.2	16.3
Costa Rica	352	83.7	45.1	24.8	18.8	16.7	16.4	16.0	17.2	18.2	19.5
Mexico	10,287	81.3	47.1	23.0	12.5	9.9	9.1	8.5	8.9	8.8	9.4
Venezuela	2,051	76.0	40.9	25.9	21.3	21.3	23.9	26.2	29.7	32.0	34.0
Peru	2,862	83.4	44.2	25.0	17.8	13.2	12.0	14.5	14.0	15.4	14.8
Middle East											
Egypt	7,252	66.0	22.8	6.7	3.3	1.9	1.8	1.2	1.2	0.9	0.8
Iran	6,566	53.2	13.3	3.8	1.2	1.1	0.9	0.8	0.8	0.6	0.6
Libya	369	26.5	8.9	2.8	1.4	0.8	0.7	<—0.6—>		<—0.6—>	
Morocco	3,299	43.5	7.5	2.9	2.1	1.3	1.7	1.5	1.8	2.6	2.4
Pakistan	23,499	25.2	5.8	2.5	1.6	1.3	1.0	1.0	0.7	0.8	---
Turkey	9,072	72.3	15.1	4.4	2.2	1.8	1.6	1.6	1.4	1.3	1.5

Sources: UN, 1964:Table 34, except for the following: Colombia [1967:Table 11]; Costa Rica [1966:Table 63]; Venezuela [1967:Table 7]; Iran [1968:Table 4]; Libya [1966:Table 27]; and Turkey [1965:Table 24].

Consequently, there is no way to estimate the actual occurrence of irregular unions. The high illegitimacy ratios in all Latin American countries suggest that such unions must far exceed official figures. For example, in 1965 illegitimacy rates in Latin America were 54 percent in Venezuela, 44 percent in Paraguay, and 43 percent in Peru [Hartley, 1969:29].

The possibility that some women living in consensual unions record themselves as married is suggested by the excess of females in the legally married category as compared to the legally married males (1.9/100 males). On the other hand, the excess of women over men reported in consensual unions (10.2/100 males) could be explained only on the assumption that women in transient sexual relationships report themselves as living in stable consensual unions [Davis, 1964:47].

The high number of single women in the Latin American population can, therefore, be accounted for by the instability of nonlegalized relationships (which are difficult to document), by postponement of marriage, and by nonmarriage. The last two factors can be documented from the information included in Table 20.

The general trend in the Latin American countries is for women to marry comparatively late. Almost one-half of all women between 20 and 24 and one-fourth between 25 and 29 are still single. Compare this to the Middle Eastern pattern in which the designation "single" begins to disappear from the population after age 25.

In all of the Latin American countries the striking incidence of nonmarriage bears greater significance than marital postponement. The regional average shows 17 percent of all adult women between ages 30 and 64 as single, with--astonishingly--almost as many in their thirties (18.8 percent) as in their sixties (19.2 percent). Evidently, the possibility for a Latin American woman past thirty to contract a union, legal or nonlegal, is very slim (Table 20).

The importance of marital postponement and of nonmarriage upon the female employment rates stems from the fact that these women provide a potential labor supply which is available at all age levels. This is, in fact, evidenced by the age-specific labor force rates of women in the Latin American countries under study, as shown in Table 18. Postponement of marriage has meant that women's withdrawal from the nonagricultural work force is not felt except in the 25 to 29 age group. In addition, by ensuring a permanent female potential available at all ages, nonmarriage reduces the age-to-age variation in employment rates in successive years after age 29, thus allowing the Latin American countries to sustain high activity rates in all age groups.

71

In most Latin American countries, taking either the total
or the urban female population as base, peak activity in nonagricultural pursuits is sustained by women within the 20 to 24 age
group. Typically, the age-specific activity rates drop between
ages 20 to 24 and 25 to 29 by four percentage points in the total
female population and by five or six percentage points in the urban
population. However, after age 30 the activity rates fluctuate
little until women reach their mid-fifties, when a general decline
in female labor force participation sets in. A contributing factor in sustaining the high age-specific activity rates at later
ages could be the influx of widowed women into the work force.
As we shall see later, however, the contribution of the single
woman is the most crucial.

In the Middle Eastern countries, despite the fact that
single women manifest a higher propensity to work than most other
marital groups, their contribution to the overall employment rates
is bound to be severely limited for the simple reason that among
populations aged 25 and above the singles form an insignificant
proportion.

Marital Fertility

Middle Eastern populations are also disadvantaged by
marital-fertility patterns. While increases in the proportion of
married women working outside the home have been related to decreas-
es in the birth rate, the relationship between the two variables
is probably more complex than a simple comparison of birth rates
would suggest. In the first place, it is the age at which women
complete their family formation rather than the ultimate size
of the family that is the deciding factor affecting the time when
women are freed from the home. In the second place, it is the
age rather than the number of children that proves to be a stronger
determinant of married women's participation in the work force.
If a woman has no children she is generally free to take a job
away from home. If she has only one small child, she is tied to
the home almost as much as if she had several [Jaffe, 1956:81;
Wolfbein and Jaffe, 1964:393]. Unfortunately, such details are
not available for all the countries under study. In fact, it is
only in Egypt and Chile that census data single out fertility performance by marital status, and only in Chile is the female labor
force cross-classified by marital status and by fertility performance. Given these limitations, marital fertility patterns
can be discussed only with reference to Chile and Egypt, and even
then the discussion will have to be restricted by information
available on the number of live-births.

Of these two countries, Egypt is evidently characterized
by higher marital fertility patterns than Chile. There is in
Chile a heavy concentration of married women in the one-to-three

parity groupings and a sharp contrast in the proportion with three children as opposed to those who have four children or more. In Egypt, the proportion of married women with five children is nearly the same as of those who have three children. Stated in more precise terms, 53 percent of all married women in Egypt have four children or more. In Chile a higher proportion, 59 percent, have three children or fewer. Also the percentage of childless wives is considerably higher in Chile than in Egypt.

The marital characteristics of Middle Eastern populations begin to take a more favorable turn for the involvement of women in the work force when the statistics on marital disruption are examined. The information included in Table 19 indicates that in the Middle East the mean-percent of women reported as previously married is higher than in the Latin American countries: the combined percent of all adult women reported as divorced/separated and widowed is 17 percent in the Middle East and only 11 percent in Latin America. The differential is not due to divorce, as may be initially expected, but to mortality differences which have left the Middle Eastern countries with a larger proportion of widowed women. It is, in fact, interesting to note that despite the practice of easy divorce in the Middle East, the average proportion of Middle Eastern women who were currently divorced at the time of the census is almost identical to the percentage reported as divorced/separated in Latin America where divorce and separation procedures are very stringent.

An apparently more decisive factor in the Middle East, however, is that women in those societies experience marital disruption, through divorce or death, at a very early age. The cross-classification of Middle Eastern populations by marital status within each specific age group shows a continual rise in the proportion of the "previously married" female group from age 35 onwards (Table 21). Typically, for the Middle East as a whole, marital disruption (without remarriage) has been experienced by 8 percent of all women by the time they attain the age bracket 35 to 39. By ages 40 to 44 the proportion has risen to 15 percent, between 45 and 49 to 23 percent, and between 55 and 59 to 38 percent. In Morocco, Pakistan, and Egypt, the incidence of disruption is much higher and occurs considerably earlier in a woman's life. For example, 30 percent of all women between ages 40 to 44 and close to 50 percent between ages 45 to 49 have lost their husbands.

In Latin American countries, by contrast, widowhood, separation, or divorce occur much later. For example, only 6 percent of all women between ages 35 to 39, 9 percent between 40 and 44, 13 percent between 45 and 49, and 25 percent between 55 and 59 have experienced terminal marital disruption.

The positive effect of this particular marital characteristic upon female employment rates lies in the availability of

TABLE 21

PERCENTAGES OF PREVIOUSLY MARRIED WOMEN AT VARIOUS AGES:
LATIN AMERICA AND THE MIDDLE EAST[a]
(c.1960)

Country	Total Aged 15+ (000s)	Age Groups									
		15-19	20-24	25-29	30-34	35-39	40-44	45-49	50-54	55-59	60-64
Latin America											
Colombia	4,843	0.4	1.8	3.0	4.9	7.1	10.8	14.7	21.3	26.5	36.2
Chile	2,306	0.2	1.2	2.6	4.4	6.7	10.2	14.5	20.8	27.9	37.3
Costa Rica	352	0.1	2.0	3.3	4.5	6.5	9.6	12.9	18.6	24.9	34.1
Mexico	10,287	0.4	1.3	2.2	5.0	7.3	11.8	15.7	22.7	27.7	40.4
Venezuela	2,051	0.2	0.8	1.4	2.8	4.2	6.8	9.5	15.8	21.3	28.5
Peru	2,862	0.3	0.9	1.8	2.7	4.8	8.2	13.1	19.3	22.9	32.0
Middle East											
Egypt	7,252	1.3	3.5	4.5	6.9	9.1	18.6	21.0	42.1	42.5	65.8
Iran	6,566	0.7	1.5	2.0	3.4	5.6	10.8	17.6	31.8	37.4	56.6
Libya	369	4.0	4.7	4.8	4.8	6.4	11.1	<—25.3—>		<—47.9—>	
Morocco	3,299	5.1	5.4	5.3	7.1	11.8	20.4	29.6	44.1	50.4	63.0
Pakistan	23,499	1.5	2.5	5.6	6.7	11.3	21.6	28.8	42.8	47.9	---
Turkey	9,072	0.3	1.1	1.6	2.4	4.2	8.0	12.4	20.1	27.2	43.5

[a]Includes widows, divorcees, and women separated from their husbands.

Sources: See Table 19.

an ever-increasing potential in the Middle Eastern labor market
from the time women are in their early forties. In Latin American countries the release of such a supply is delayed until women
are in their early fifties. The age-specific labor force rates
for Iran, Morocco, Pakistan, Turkey, and Libya suggest evidence
of such a trend. In these five countries there is a continual
rise in the female employment curve after age 35, peaking in the
middle or advanced ages. The propensity for women to be nonagricultural labor force members is highest between ages 35 and 50
in Turkey, 40 and 54 in Libya, 35 and 54 in Pakistan, 35 and 60
in Morocco, and 40 and 55 in Iran. Although the data available
do not allow a precise isolation of specific-age-group in the
labor force by marriage status, it is probable (given the universality of marriage in those societies) that such a pattern
reflects the influx of widowed and divorced women into the labor
market.

The discussion has highlighted important differences between Latin American and Middle Eastern societies with respect to
family characteristics centrally related to women's work participation. It is possible now to take these findings a step further
and to examine the extent to which such intrinsic differences are
in actuality responsible for the regional disparity in female
employment rates.

Other conditions being equal, it is reasonable to expect
that the positive effect of a late marriage/nonmarriage syndrome
upon the female labor force rates in Latin America would be counterbalanced by the positive effect of a frequent-and-early incidence of marital disruption upon women's employment rates in the
Middle East. If this were so, a certain levelling in activity
rates between the two sets of countries would emerge. But in
actuality the frequency of widowhood and divorce in the Middle
East has not increased female employment rates to equal those in
the Latin American countries. Could it be, then, that the particular family characteristics prevailing in Latin America outweigh
those of the Middle East insofar as the involvement of women in
the labor force is concerned?

One way to test this possibility is to examine what would
happen to the overall female participation rates in the Middle
Eastern countries if women in those societies assumed the same
marital structure as their counterparts in Latin America; and
conversely, what would happen in Latin America if women were subjected to the age-by-marriage distribution typical of the female
population in the Middle East.

75

The Influence of Family Characteristics Upon Women's
Employment Rates

In the remaining part of this chapter, the discussion
focuses upon the results obtained through standardization analysis
in testing the effects of population differences upon the female
employment rates.

Table 22 shows the effect of standardizing the female
labor force rates of Turkey and Syria by the marital status
structure of Colombia and Peru, respectively. To be able to
isolate the specific influence yielded by population differences
for Middle Eastern women, it was necessary to hold the actual
activity rates within each marital group constant. Assuming then
that the propensity to work by marital status remains unchanged
in Turkey and Syria, the results obtained in Table 22 indicate
the number of Middle Eastern women "expected" to be in the nonagricultural labor force, if in those societies the marital distribution of the female population is similar to that of Colombia
and Peru respectively. The table shows clearly that in the Middle
East the impact of a change in marital structure is minimal.
Standardizing the female labor force rates of Turkey by the marital distribution of Colombia has raised the Turkish rates by a
meager margin from 2.3 to 3.6 percentage points. Similarly, when
Syrian women are given the marital-structure of Peru, the expected
activity rate is only 1.1 percentage points higher than the actual.
Considering that the discrepancy between any of these two sets of
countries ranges from 17 to 20 percent, the increase registered
through standardization leaves a substantial regional differential
unexplained.

As is to be expected, the standardization of Middle Eastern
women by the marital structure of Latin America yields a consistent
increase in the number of single women in the hypothetical population and a corresponding decrease in the number of married and
widowed. When the expected effects of marital differences are
compared to the actual female labor force, the number of single
women is raised by 135,000 in Turkey and by 18,000 in Syria.
Normally such an increase would trigger a considerable rise in
the overall female employment rates. However, the gain in single
women is offset by the substantial loss of married and widowed
women from the expected labor force count.

Standardization analysis also points to the negative influence of differences due to marital-fertility patterns. The
observed fertility-specific activity rate of Chilean wives is reduced from 10.7 to 9.4 percent when Chilean wives are subjected
to Egypt's marital-fertility schedule. The labor force rate of
the married female population in Egypt is 1.4 percentage points;
the standardization procedure therefore leaves a balance of 8.2
percentage points as yet unexplained.

TABLE 22

TURKEY AND SYRIA: MARITAL-SPECIFIC ACTIVITY RATES OF
FEMALE WORKERS, ACTUAL AND STANDARDIZED BY
OTHER-COUNTRY MARITAL DISTRIBUTIONS

Country and Marital State	Actual Population			Expected Population Standardized by Marital Distribution		
	Marital Distribution	Workers	Activity Rates	Standardized	Expected Workers	Expected Overall Rate
Syria: *Standardized by Marital Distribution of Peru*						
Total[a]	1,137,460	32,631	2.8	1,137,460	44,379	3.9
Single	162,790	13,957	8.6	371,949	31,987	
Married	810,376	12,620	1.5	657,452	9,861	
Widowed	146,102	3,278	2.2	102,372	2,047	
Divorced	9,584	814	8.5	5,687	484	
Turkey: *Standardized by Marital Distribution of Colombia*						
Total[a]	9,062,056	210,400	2.3	9,062,056	325,951	3.6
Single	1,319,279	85,099	6.5	3,380,147	219,709	
Married	6,594,359	93,286	1.4	4,775,703	66,859	
Widowed	1,064,474	19,161	1.8	734,027	13,212	
Divorced	83,944	12,759	15.2	172,179	26,171	

[a]Totals exclude women of unknown marital status

Sources: Syria, 1962:Table 42; UN 1969:Table 7.
Turkey, 1965:Tables 24, 44; UN 1969:Table 7.

Since marital-status structure and marital-fertility in themselves are not decisive in accounting for the regional dissimilarity in female employment rates, conclusive determinants must be found elsewhere. Since women's accession to or withdrawal from the labor force at certain ages are largely determined by shifts in the life cycle, it follows that the age at which these shifts are most intimately connected with their work-participation bears positively upon their propensity to be employed. The pronounced differences between Latin American and Middle Eastern societies with respect to variables such as age-at-marriage, age-at-widowhood, and divorce have been demonstrated in Tables 20 and 21. It remains to test whether these factors are more dominant than marital status structure alone in accounting for the dissimilarity in women's employment rates.

In the following analyses the flow of influences has been reversed in the sense that standardization procedures test the influence yielded by population differences upon female employment rates *in the Latin American countries*. Accordingly, Table 23 shows the effects of subjecting the female population of Chile and Ecuador to the age-by-marriage distribution of six Middle Eastern countries: Libya, Morocco, Egypt, Pakistan, Turkey, and Iran. The analysis could not be extended to the other Latin American countries under study because of insufficient data from which to compute the female age-specific marital-specific employment rates.

The results presented in Table 23 show that the age-by-marriage distribution pattern of the Middle East does operate in a limited way to depress the female employment rates. However, the loss incurred through standardization is not expansive enough to explain the regional discrepancies. The female employment rates in Chile, to cite one example, drop from 23.2 to approximately 15 percent when standardized by Morocco and Libya and to 19 percent when standardized by Egypt and Pakistan. Yet the actual differential in female activity rates between Chile and these four countries ranges between 19 and 21 percent.

Additional confirmation of the fallibility of this variable is provided by urban population analysis. When the age-specific/marital-specific labor force rates of urban women in Ecuador are standardized by the age-at-marriage distribution of urban Turkey and urban Iran, the actual employment rate of Ecuador, which is 28.3 percent, is reduced to only 22.2 and 21.0 percent respectively. In absolute terms, the initial number of urban female workers drops upon standardization from an original 132,500 to 99,722 and 94,193 respectively. Bearing in mind that the difference in urban activity rates between Ecuador and these two Middle Eastern countries is 19 percent, the above explanation proves inadequate (Table 23).

TABLE 23

CHILE AND URBAN ECUADOR: MARITAL-SPECIFIC ACTIVITY RATES OF
FEMALE WORKERS, ACTUAL AND STANDARDIZED BY
OTHER-COUNTRY AGE-AT-MARRIAGE

		Total Women Aged 15–64	Age Groups					
			15–24	25–34	35–44	45–54	55–64	
Chile								
Actual rates		*23.2*	*28.0*	*25.9*	*22.4*	*20.4*	*15.3*	
Standardized by:	Morocco	14.7	8.8	15.6	20.9	19.8	14.4	
	Libya	14.9	12.9	14.7	18.0	17.6	13.0	
	Egypt	19.0	19.1	16.5	20.3	19.6	13.9	
	Pakistan	18.0	18.5	17.7	18.2	17.9	14.6	
Urban Ecuador								
Actual rates		*28.3*	*32.5*	*28.4*	*24.5*	*22.7*	*21.2*	
Standardized by:	Urban Turkey	22.2	27.6	20.9	19.2	18.1	15.3	
	Urban Iran	21.0	24.4	20.1	18.7	17.8	18.7	

Sources: UN, 1963:Table 34; Chile, 1964:Tables 18, 20; Ecuador, 1964:
Tables 6, 9; Turkey, 1969:Table 24; Iran, 1966:Table 5.

The Female Potential in the Middle East

In Middle Eastern societies the supply of women available to the labor force is clearly not a function of the marital and fertility characteristics of the female population. This explains why, when Middle Eastern women were subjected through standardization procedures to marital conditions highly conducive to a large-scale involvement in the work force, they persisted in displaying very low activity rates. By the same token, standardizing the Latin American activity rates by the Middle Eastern family characteristics did not yield the expected decline in participation rates either.

Both these findings introduce a new dimension to the variables related to female labor force behavior. Explanations for the regional divergencies in work force involvement have to be sought in the motivational and social contexts within those societies.

That motivational factors rather than marital characteristics lie at the root of the regional variation can be tested by turning the problem around and asking what--given the current family characteristics of the Middle East--would be the womanpower potential if in those societies the female propensity to be employed were similar to conditions in Latin America?

To test this possibility, we shall assume that all of the adult women in Libya, Egypt, Morocco, and Pakistan manifest the same propensity to be employed within each specific age group, by marriage class, as women do in Chile. This allows an estimation of the number of potential female workers in the four countries given their present marital distribution within each specific age group. The results of this "experiment" are presented in Table 24. Holding the current marital characteristics of the female population constant, Morocco has the potential to effect a *three-fold* increase in the nonagricultural female activity rates; each of Libya and Egypt a *five-fold* increase; and Pakistan a *seven-fold* increase.

80

TABLE 24

LIBYA, EGYPT, PAKISTAN, AND MOROCCO: AGE-SPECIFIC ACTIVITY RATES OF
WOMEN, STANDARDIZED BY AGE-MARITAL-SPECIFIC RATES OF CHILE
(Total Population)

Country	Total Women Aged 15-64	Age Groups									
		15-19	20-24	25-29	30-34	35-39	40-44	45-49	50-54	55-59	60-64
Libya											
Actual	3.0	7.8	3.4	3.0	3.2	3.3	3.7	← 3.7 →		← 2.5 →	↑
Expected	15.2	11.9	14.0	14.6	14.9	15.0	21.1	← 17.9 →		← 13.2 →	
Egypt											
Actual	3.1	4.4	4.9	3.0	2.5	2.4	2.9	2.5	2.8	2.1	1.9
Expected	17.2	14.4	19.1	16.4	16.5	16.5	23.6	18.3	20.3	14.1	12.5
Pakistan											
Actual	2.2	1.4	1.8	← 2.1 →		← 2.7 →		← 2.8 →		← 2.5 →	
Expected	15.7	10.9	12.0	14.2	15.8	17.3	24.6	20.2	20.5	15.3	---
Morocco											
Actual	5.7	5.5	5.2	← 4.9 →		← 6.4 →		← 7.2 →		← 6.3 →	
Expected	16.7	15.4	13.6	← 15.5 →		← 20.8 →		← 20.6 →		← 13.6 →	

Chapter 6

THE ROLE OF THE FAMILY IN THE STRUCTURE OF SOCIAL CHANGE

A definitive explanation for the regional differences in
employment rates has yet to be found despite the variety of ap-
proaches taken thus far. Clearly, the root cause or causes must
be sought in forces outside the traditionally invoked variables
related to labor supply and labor demand. The angle of approach
in this chapter is that the regional divergency in feminine
employment is in large part due to the different conditions under
which systems of social control have developed in Latin American
and Middle Eastern countries.

Three major questions arise. *Who* controls the decision
over women's work participation in these two societies? *Why* are
women controlled? *How* is this control exercised?

Within the context of broad comparative analysis, the
following discussion deals with regional variations in the
structure of social control, their sources, and their consequences
by singling out significant analogies and equally significant
differences between the machinery of social control in Latin
America and the Middle East. A useful point at which to begin
this comparison is the institutional and normative contexts governing family organization in the two regions since family is the
prime instrumental agency through which social control is exercised, particularly with respect to women.

Family "Honor" and Social Control

It is difficult to find a clear foundation for the difference in feminine behavior between Latin America and the Middle East in the cultural prescriptions of kinship structures.
The normative patterns governing family organization are practically identical in both societies, which is not surprising in
view of the historical relationship between the two cultures.
The linking feature can be found in the institutional structure
of Latin America, which by being Spanish carries a substantial
Muslim influence. The 800 years or so of Moorish hegemony over
Spain ended at about the time Spanish America was discovered.
It is conceivable that many of the cultural patterns introduced

into the new land by the Spanish conquistadores reflected the
value system developed in the Iberian peninsula through contact
with the Moors [Warshaw, 1922:282].

Both Latin America and the Middle East have traditionally
sanctioned institutional structures noted for their strong
familism, patriarchialism, male supremacy, and an established
religion (Catholicism in one, Islam in the other) which reinforce
the subordinate position of women in the social structure. In
both societies, familial organization is the base of social order.
Family considerations control the behavior of people because in
the social contexts of both regions the main source of individual
identity lies within the family rank [Adams, 1967:156-160; Hammel,
1961:989-1005; Adams et al., 1960:33-34; Patai, 1955; Rivlin and
Szyliowicz, 1965:25].

Obviously, Latin America and the Middle East also share
many of the ideal normative patterns of personal and family honor.
In both societies the criterion of family esteem depends largely
if not exclusively upon conformity to behavioral norms that are
conceived as touching upon male honor. Male honor is symbolized
in the idea of two sex-linked characteristics that distinguish
the ideal character of men and women: the manliness of man
(machismo, muruwwa) and the sexual purity of woman (vergüenza,
'ird). Both concepts are at the highest level of cultural valuation and have a clear structural meaning. They reflect a solid
corpus of values which control behavior and act as effective
checks on social relationships.

The concept of honor influences both the division of
labor and the division of roles within the family. To the
dominant male is ascribed the combination of power, authority,
and sexual bravado coupled with the defense and protection of
female purity. Women are frail, helpless, weak, and unable to
govern and protect their sexuality without the defense of the men
of their families. The male of the family, as father, husband,
or brother, is responsible for guarding the female's sexual honor.
If her reputation is besmirched, the stigma of immoral or unmanly
behavior falls upon *him*. He must ensure respect for the women
of his household and maintain the defense mechanisms safeguarding
his womenfolk from the outside world. His own sexual freedom
is assured, but he must be always on guard against the aggression
of other—equally free—males toward the women of *his* family. His
defense may go to the extreme of risking human life: his own,
that of the intruder, and possibly even that of the honor-threaten-
ing woman. Charles Issawi, in discussing the vigor of this defense,
notes that in the Middle East "the feeling that a woman so funda-
mentally belongs to the male members of the household that any
misbehavior on her part stains the honor of her father, brother
or husband is so strong that every year witnesses hundreds of
murders often in circumstances of great cruelty designed to wipe
out the stain" [1947:159-160].

Two comments from the Latin American sphere show that this role ideal is equally deeply stamped into the feminine fiber of South American women. The De Hoyos have noted that "Observers have wondered why Mexican women, especially wives, are often conspicuous for their absence in public life, and social functions. It is never clear whether Mexican men are ashamed of their women, think of their women as hindering them socially or feel their women to be out of place" [1966:106ff]. And Hanke observed that "Despite the Revolution in Mexico, there have been no successful efforts to sweep from the feminine mind the preconceptions about her incapacity, her dependence on man and her absolute need for resignation that traditionally weighed her down for centuries" [1968:221-222; see also Simic, 1969:89-100; Berger, 1964:113; Rivlin, 1965:35].

An inevitable correlate of this concept of honor is the submissive role ascribed to the woman and the unmistakable suspicion with which she is regarded lest by her overt actions or her inability to protect herself she put a blot upon the family. The ideal woman is sexually pure, submissive, and obedient to authority of the male. She is expected to defer to her father, brothers, and husband, to serve dutifully in the home, to acquire no education outside the home, and to seek no advancement beyond that inherent in the roles promulgated by her kinsmen.

The historical causes at the root of this deep suspicion of women have not been investigated for either the Middle East or Latin America. Neither has any systematic attempt been made to trace the infiltration of Muslim sex norms (through the Moors and Turks) into Spain and other Mediterranean countries, despite the existence of the same general ideological patterns regarding family honor and the expectations of male and female behavior in almost all Mediterranean countries, the Balkans, and the Arab Middle East.

Several tentative explanations can be advanced for the Middle East. In early Arabia the danger of sexual infidelity may have been real. Trading caravans enforced prolonged absences of men from their homes and left women unguarded. Then again, during early Islam the practice of slavery and exchange of concubines probably led men to regard women as defenseless sexual objects. The deep suspicion of women in the Middle East has also been related to the concept of sex in Islam. Robert Bellah writes:

> The realm of sexual relations has been viewed as one to be regulated and controlled rather than given positive meaning. Associated with this attitude has been a deep suspicion of women. Without external restraints, it was felt, their sexual relations would run wild. This may be more folk belief than religious

teaching, but the latter has on the whole reinforced the former [1968:33].

Given such a normative framework, a series of institutional arrangements is predictable. Primarily, a social system in which the security of a man's honor lies in the sexual virtue of his womenfolk is bound to engender within its very structure rules controlling the relationship between the sexes and an effective mechanism of positive and negative sanctioning which would ensure the enforcement of such rules. It is, therefore, to be expected that concern with sexual purity and the high cultural value placed on virginity would lead to the practice of early and parentally supervised marriage and to the relative seclusion of adolescent girls before that event. Marital fidelity would be supposedly maintained by an asymmetric role structure which defines the woman's role as explicitly subsidiary to that of the husband, confines the wife to the home and children, and restricts her social life to the company of other female relatives.

Since honor is protected effectively by conforming in every outward aspect of behavior to a code of sexual shame, differentiation of sex role behavior is expected to be maximized to the extent that it advocates exclusion of women from participation in public life. Because social intermingling of the sexes is looked upon with suspicion, it is understandable that education and occupation are expected to compromise a girl's sex ethics and to threaten her eventual chances of marriage. Female participation in such spheres would ultimately engineer a reconsideration of the overall relationships between men and women.

In Middle Eastern societies most of these expectations are being met. The existing institutional arrangements and their cultural adjuncts have been effective in cementing the syndrome of family honor and female chastity by confining women to the home and barring them from involvement in alternatives to marriage and childbearing. Although there are significant class differences in the Middle East in the nature and extent of women's seclusion from participation in public activities, for the bulk of the population the structures, attitudes, and practices reinforcing the cultural definition of the female role are maintained by societal edicts.

What has just been said, however, hardly applies in practice to the Latin American countries where feminine behavior varies significantly from normative expectations. For how, otherwise, can one reconcile statements regarding the cultural definition of the female role in those societies with the widespread employment of women? This incongruity requires further elucidation.

Challenges to Kinship Control

In Latin America one of the mainsprings for the apparent
discrepancy between "ideal" and "real" behavior is that the
machinery of social control over women is neither institutionally
strong nor tightly integrated. Given the cultural valuation
placed upon male honor in the community it is to be expected that
in both Latin America and the Middle East the performance of
social control over women be delegated to and assumed exclusively
by male members of the family group. This expectation is a natural
outcome of the importance of family organization in the social
structure and of the assertion that the security of family honor
is vested in the sexual virtue of the womenfolk.

Kinship institutions in the Middle East effectively implement social control. A strong kin network, in conjunction with
other social institutions, keeps women in tight control. In Latin
America, by contrast, outside forces have challenged the importance of the family as an agent of social control. Male authority
over family females has either collapsed or been weakened, and the
male prerogative to restrain and censure them has been attenuated.

The application of this framework suggests three major
questions. First, have certain historical or social conditions
peculiar to Latin America challenged the characteristic system
of family control? Second, in what particular way did these
forces operate to circumvent the institutionalization of ideal
family norms? Third, what, by contrast, are some of the structur-
ing factors in Middle Eastern societies which have served to
keep the normative prescriptions of kinship institutions functioning? The thrust of the remaining portion of this chapter is
directed toward answering these questions.

The Impact of the Spanish Conquest.--Among the several
paths of causation that have thwarted the institutionalization of
normative behavior in Latin America and challenged the importance
of the family in the system of social control, two factors are
singled out for discussion. First is the complexity of the
Spanish conquest which brought about deep ethnic cleavages in
Latin America and prevented the social and cultural integration
of the indigenous population into the dominant system of norms.
Second is the distinctive system of religious organization in
Latin America, specifically the Catholic clergy who have evolved
a competitive role for themselves with regard to kinsmen and
subsequently reduced the extent to which women are subjected to
the authority of the family.

The importance of the Spanish conquest derives from its
association with (a) the destruction of aboriginal frameworks
and the downfall of cultures and societies existing in America
before Columbus, (b) an incomplete socio-cultural integration,

and (c) a clear-cut hierarchy among ethnic groups which has resulted in a rigidly stratified caste society [Houtart and Pin, 1965:5,12,30; Stavenhagen, 1970:266-270]. The combination of these factors created a distinct type of family behavior among the indigenous population, who are at the bottom of the socio-economic scale, in marked contrast with the system of kinship organization characteristic of the Spanish-descended middle and upper social groups [Azevedo, 1965:296; Adams, 1967:153; Willems, 1953:338].

Within a century of their landing in America, the Spanish had succeeded in undermining native social and cultural organizations by the steady economic and political pressures of a closed-class system. Social solidarity was fractionated by the forced dispersion of large segments of the native population under the *repartimiento* and *encomienda* systems; traditional religious institutions were abolished, to be replaced by some form of Catholicism, and the family unit was severely threatened as local women became part of the booty of conquest.

Hand in hand with the disintegration of the indigenous social system was the deliberate action taken by the Spaniards to prevent the absorption of the native population into that of the colonizing group. The arrangement of a rigidly stratified caste society became clear within a few years after the conquest. At the top of the scale were the Spaniards (the Peninsulares) followed by the Creoles (the Spanish born in America). At the lower end were the mestizo (mixed Spanish and Amerindian) and the mulatto (mixed Negro and European). This caste system was sustained by a rigid colonial policy which forbade to the lower social groups the usual rewards of cultural assimilation and high social mobility. The locus of all political and economic power remained in Spanish hands: the church accepted Indians as parishioners, not as priests. Steady economic and political pressures were directed toward keeping the conquered docile, not toward transforming them. Short of religious conversion, few attempts were made to indoctrinate the Indian with Spanish norms and cultural values. This meant that for many generations the indigenous population was left without an internally integrated system of values with which they could identify. The Spaniards had not only truncated the traditional social values of the Indian; they subsequently offered him very little prospect of ever being integrated into the dominant culture of the ruling group [Goode, 1964:30; Houtart and Pin, 1965:14]. The repercussions of such a cultural breakdown upon family organization were considerable.

Because the conquerors were too few to guarantee the loss of identity of the great mass of Indians, the Spanish implemented a long and widespread miscegenation in the hope that its consequences would outlast the severance of political links [Andreski, 1969:156-159]. Historically, few Spaniards married their Indian

87

sexual companions or supported them and the numerous offspring from this unregulated interbreeding. For the most part, the Spanish conquest is associated with the sexual exploitation of local women and the massive propagation of children stigmatized by illegitimacy and not fully recognized by the world of either parent [Herring, 1961:188; Schurz, 1954:299; Goode, 1961:910-925].

Under such circumstances it is easy to see how the Spanish policy of miscegenation may have generated a considerable amount of social displacement and incongruency of status within the indigenous family unit and undermined the authority of family members. What fragmentary evidence we possess of Indian social organization before the Spanish conquest documents the importance of the family in the institutional structure and the strong disapproval of illegitimacy [Goode, 1971:476; Herring, 1961:46, 55]. Marriage was safeguarded by a rigorous code, which, although it permitted polygamy and divorce (at least for the Aztecs), protected the rights of women and placed them in definite positions within the kinship and social structure. Under the conditions of conquest, however, the marriage bond lost its significance and so did the prestige and authority of family members. Where women are treated as part of the spoils of conquest, male elders (the presupposed guardians of family honor) are hard put to protect their womenfolk, nor can they impose sanctions for transgressions. Any attempt to censure their women's conduct would have served only to emphasize their tragically ridiculous impotence before the conquerors.

Unfortunately, the social influence of Spanish colonization continued to persist in Latin America even after independence was achieved. The sexual and marital patterns characteristic of the urban lower classes today reflect the inability of the family to outgrow the historical legacy of female concubinage. Men have not regained control over their womenfolk. Sexual freedom is prevalent, and illegitimacy rates are high, because family controls are inadequate to enforce sexual chastity or to pressure a man to marry a pregnant girl. As a consequence, the sanctions against illicit sexual relations, consensual unions, and birth out of wedlock cannot be invoked effectively.

The lower classes continue to be exploited politically and economically and their women, particularly in urban areas, have remained part of an inter-trade system. The historical relationship between conquerors and conquered has been supplanted by an embittered relationship between classes in which wealthy men feel entitled to the sexual services of lower-class women. This attitude extends to the occupational world where an employer will not hesitate to use economic pressure to ensure the sexual compliance of women working under him [Andreski, 1969:50]. The main difference between colonial and present conditions is that today the lower-class woman is taken advantage of not only by men who belong to the upper social groups but also by men of her own rank.

The inability of the lower-class family to reassert its powers of control stems from two sources. One, the economically deprived feel that they have little honor to lose, hence the motivation among men to impose restraint upon their women's conduct is weak. Two, male relatives have difficulty in supervising their women even when they want to, either because they are absent from the home or because girls are employed. This can thwart the most effective way of protecting young women from being exploited. A family situation where a male relative is at all times available to retaliate if a daughter or a sister has been molested will advertise to intruders that a virgin is not to be tempted [Blake, 1962:89].

The absence of family controls, whether by choice or by necessity, has meant that courtship takes place anonymously without the supervision of an adult or adolescent peer. Since no normative conditions are set for this interaction, the girl is forced to establish an individual role bargain with the man.

The Role of the Catholic Clergy.--Granted that historical circumstances tended to circumvent some of the ideal normative patterns of family organization among the lower classes, we still must account for family behavior among the rest of the population. For example, how closely associated is the behavior of the upper class woman in Latin America with the ideological patterns regarding the feminine role?

The general contention has been that in Latin America the privileged strata have preserved many of the cultural values and traditional behavior introduced by the Spanish gentry. This is clearly reflected in the importance of the kinship group among the middle and upper classes in which family bonds exert considerable control over behavior. One of the major reasons why kinship units have been able to maintain their primacy in the higher social structure is the distinct advantages that individual members derive from family networks. Since up until now the main source of social and individual identity has lain within the family rank, the middle and upper class has depended upon family position in all matters related to social prestige, political influence, and the protection of property. Concern for the protection of family rank within the community has sustained the legal dominance of the male in family relationships and reinforced his power of authority. The traditional concept of family honor has remained a crucial determinant of social esteem, and the male has been the recognized guardian of family status. Hence one finds definite structures and attitudes which maintain and reinforce the subsidiary position of women before and during marriage [McGinnis, 1966:25-31; Gutierrez de Pineda, 1964:440].

Careful consideration of the behavior of middle and upper class women, however, shows that this ideal position may be more apparent than real. The relatively high educational standard of women and their substantial participation in the upgraded occupations suggest that the upper class female is not as secluded as we are led to believe, nor is she strictly circumscribed to the traditional role of marriage and childbearing. Interestingly enough, answers to some of the questions related to the growing emancipation of Latin American women and their emergence in public life are intimately connected with the Catholic Church.

The sociological features of the church as a formal organization and the role of the clergy as a dimension of the variables that have challenged the importance of the kinship unit are elusive. The tendency to underline the conservative influence of the church in bolstering traditional family values and in upholding the subordinate role ascribed to women tends to overlook the equally important historical fact that clerical organizations are "competitive with kinship groups for loyalty, personnel and property" [Blake, 1967:135]. In the particular case of Latin America, women's close and frequent association with the church has led to the clergy's evolvement of a competitive role vis-à-vis the family unit which has operated to dilute the control exercised by kinsmen over their womenfolk.

To appreciate fully why and how this challenge came about, it is necessary to trace the historical position of the Catholic clergy in the social structure of Latin America from pre-independence times.

Ecclesiastical power in Latin America was an essential feature of Spanish colonialism. During the three centuries of colonial rule the church was an indispensable ally of the Spanish crown in subjugating the Indian population. It also supplied officials in the colonial administration and enforced centripetal tendencies among the Spanish settlers who, without this binding force, might have fractionated the empire [Andreski, 1969:188].

From the outset, the symbols of religious authority went hand in hand with political maneuvering. Naturally, relations between church and state varied with differing circumstances in the republics, but the overriding trend was that the church always aligned itself with political power and secured its legal basis of support and dominance from political elites [Vallier, 1970:34]. As long as the church held an assured position in society it felt little need to channel its efforts into building religious solidarity or developing specialized instruments of religious control. However, under post-independence political conditions the whole problem of the church-state relationship took on a new dimension as the church lost many sources of its derivative power as well as its political and economic base of operation.

Following the declaration of independence the formal separation of state and church was reached by varying stages. In certain instances priests were banned from holding public office. In others the state took over all activities traditionally in the hands of the church, such as controlling vital statistics, handling educational enterprises, and running hospitals and charitable institutions. In some countries the church lost even the power to control the contraction or the dissolution of marriages [Pike, 1964:13].

In addition to the loss of most of its prerogatives, the church was also threatened during the post-independence period by an outbreak of strong anticlerical feelings among large and influential sectors of the population. Several factors contributed to this tide. Originating in colonial times because of the antinationalist record of the church, anticlericalism became intensified in the nineteenth and twentieth centuries when new middle groups began to challenge the old landowning elite for political supremacy. Among the middle sector the clergy was resented strongly, not only because it sided with the customary elites (the landed aristocracy), but also because of the economic privileges that the church enjoyed. After the confiscation of the royal domains the church remained the biggest landowner, and appetite for its lands stimulated anticlericalism even among the traditional aristocrats. By immobilizing enormous areas of real property and hoarding precious metal, the church also incurred hostility within commercial circles because it acted as a brake on the development of business enterprises [Houtart and Pin, 1965:35; Andreski, 1969:189-190].

Anticlericalism in Latin America was further spurred by widespread reports depicting priests as seducers of women. The profligacy of the Catholic priesthood in Latin America is well documented in the literature--the clergy appears to have been the most licentious in the world. Clerical concubinage was so common in that region that it became accepted by the public as normal behavior [D'Antonio and Pike, 1964:64; Schurz, 1963:262].

All these factors combined were sufficiently strong to engender rejection of the clergy and, eventually, of the sacramental role of the church itself. The relationship of the bulk of the population to the church had for a long time been tenuous enough to foster the emergence of a religion grossly aberrant from Catholic dogma with little place for priests and the holy sacraments. The eruption of anticlericalism among the middle sector, which was gradually rising to political prominence, clearly meant that the only source of support left to the church was the hereditary aristocracy [D'Antonio and Pike, 1964:9].

As Vallier has so aptly stated, the Latin American Catholic Church in the post-independence period had lost its potential to generate commitments in terms of loyalties, resources, and behavioral support by invoking its capacities as a religious system. Fully conscious of its lack of an autonomous religious strength from which to operate, the church instituted a new strategy. This was to build up and channel membership-based religious enthusiasm through borrowed microstructures such as the Catholic labor organizations, trade unions, parochial schools and universities, cultural centers and youth clubs. In addition, the priesthood embarked on a policy of multiple involvements in nonecclesiastical units such as the family, the local communities, and the aristocratic circles. These social institutions, as they became fully integrated into the Catholic religion, not only abided by the ethics and natural law as taught by the church, but actively promoted the church's religious norms [Vallier, 1967:193].

The establishment of these "catholic" institutions guaranteed the church access to the new generation. Close contact with the aristocracy, the community, and the family provided the clergy with an enormous base for the mobilization of religious proselityzers who could serve as apostles for the church by transmitting religious doctrine and assuring Christian conformity in daily life. From among the primary groups tapped by the clergy to function as an organized system of catechetical instruction none equalled the family. And within the family unit, it was the woman, particularly in her mother-role, who was selected as the special microagent entrusted with the task of achieving and perpetuating religious influence. Hence women were strategically important to the vested interests of the clergy. Together with other microstructures the female element had come to represent an important lay apostolate who could help the church regain prominence.

This attempt to link church and society through women entailed the development of effective channels through which to control and supervise the female stratum. The most far-reaching influence achieved in this direction was through religious ritual. Confession, in particular, allowed priests to establish especially close channels of communication with women and, eventually, to propagate their own patronage and control. Although men were nominal Catholics, the sex differentials in overt church participation in Latin American countries were significant. Women, particularly members of the middle and upper classes, made up the majority of faithful attendants at mass, at confession, and at communion. Clerical control was undoubtedly strengthened by the socially sanctioned "double standard" characterizing the marriage relationship among the middle and upper social groups. The clergy managed to draw full advantage from the shifting balance of power as women, disappointed in their marriages, turned to religion for help and comfort.[1]

---

[1]For amplification of sex differentials in church participation, refer to Schurz, 1954:334; Houtart and Pin, 1965:172-174; D'Antonio

The church used a more direct means to intensify its influence over women by establishing parochial secondary schools and universities, both of which bolstered higher female education. It has been estimated that more than one-third of the entire educational system in Latin America is run by the church. This is despite initial state control over educational enterprises in the period immediately following independence. The church operates 60 percent of all secondary schools which account for an average of 50 percent of the enrollment, although in some countries this figure runs as high as 80 percent. In addition, there are several Catholic universities. Both schools and universities are particularly appealing to middle and upper class girls because they provide social and racial segregation.

Understandably, church efforts in the direction of reinforcing religious loyalty among the female stratum have been confined to members of the privileged social groups. It is, after all, only from among the upper echelons of society that the church can hope to draw political and financial support and to recruit a selective student body for its exclusive private schools. Further, since among the upper classes the family unit still operates as a milieu of control for the individual and upon which he depends for status, it is among such groups that the effectiveness of the family as an organized system of religious instruction is most likely to succeed.

It is almost certain that the institutional strategy followed by the clergy was not intended to "liberate" the middle and upper class woman. Nevertheless, the Latin American woman has reaped distinct advantages from it. Once upper class women were recognized as a major source of support, the church felt obliged to establish meaningful rewards for this group as a means of drawing them into religious responsibility. The association of religiosity with privileges was accentuated in several ways: in addition to being "granted" the privilege of higher education in exclusive schools and universities, women were also "allowed" to distribute charity, to "organize" church-sponsored activities and to "offer" catechetical instruction.

In time what were at the outset only special privileges for the few developed into legitimate educational and occupational opportunities for middle and upper class women at large. By fostering female involvement in religious, educational, and civic spheres, the clergy had inadvertently provided women with legitimate alternatives to their traditional roles in the fields of teaching, social welfare, and other professional specialization. Such a situation assured the woman of a status and an identity outside the family nexus and enabled her to overcome the socially engendered limitations prescribed by tradition.

---

and Pike, 1964:62,256; Vallier, 1970:30.

The clergy enhanced the position of middle and upper class women in one other related way. Although these groups of women were traditionally subjected to the full authority and control of male family members, today, because of the pervasive sway of the clergy over women, control is shared among two competing male groups: kinsmen and clergymen. The ability of the priesthood to become part of the structure of control has diluted the authority of the family and kept male members from completely dominating the existence of their women. As a consequence the prerogative of men to impose censure and restrictions on their women has been shaken. Women have naturally benefited from the break-up of the monolithic structure. They are now able to play off the two authorities, one against the other, and to reap the benefits of the alternatives that are made available to them in the process.

The Machinery of Social Control in the Middle East

In the Middle East and Latin America the machinery of social control contrasts sharply. Middle Eastern kinship networks have remained traditionally strong to the extent that they monopolize the function of social control. No other institution has emerged to challenge the authority of male family members or even to question it. Female seclusion is legitimized in terms of family honor and is implemented in actuality. The cultural importance of chastity is reflected in the social system through institutional arrangements which keep women from participating in public activities which presuppose contact with the opposite sex. Among the more significant indicators of the tight control exercised over women are the practice of parentally arranged marriages, male/female segregation in post-primary levels in public and private schools (excepting the university), and sex-segregated activities in the labor market and in most social activities.

It is necessary now to attempt to identify some of the cultural and historical forces in the Middle Eastern world which have helped to sustain the primacy of kinship controls. Three major influences are discussed: (a) the historical conditions of the Muslim conquest; (b) the "nature" of Islam as a religious system; and (c) the absence of an organized clergy in Islam.

The Arab-Muslim Conquest.--The rhythm of the Arab-Muslim penetration into the Middle Eastern countries is inverse to that of the Spaniards into Latin America. Starting as a provincial community, the Arabs quickly advocated a universal religion and implemented a political organization dominating half the civilized world. More astonishing than the speed of the Arab conquest was its orderly character. Although under the early Omayyad period Islam presented itself merely to members of the Arab race as a great unifying principle, under Abbasside rule its wider conquests led to its becoming a tremendous force for wiping out tribal, national, and racial distinctions on a world scale [Hitti, 1967:287].

94

The vastness of the areas conquered by the Muslims confronted the nomadic Arab with a staggering task--through political control to unify populations characterized not only by extensive ethnic heterogeneity but also by a diversity of cultures far superior to his own. Despite this, the Arab conquest succeeded in creating a striking unity or similarity of sentiments and attitudes among all Muslims both within themselves and vis-à-vis the non-Muslims which has justified the concept: the Muslim world.

The source of this unification has to be sought in the early processes of arabicization and islamization [Witteck, 1938: 38; Blachere, 1956:256]. Far from working on a monolithic principle of standardization, Islam operated on a principle of toleration and absorption of a vast diversity of cultural patterns and social practices. With the subjugation of highly civilized peoples, the Arab conquerors freely melded diverse elements from local cultures into their own institutions and laws. At the same time they impressed upon everything they acquired the unmistakable stamp of Islam. As long as the local traditions and customs of the new converts fitted into the broad world-view of Islam, they were legitimized and integrated into the main corpus of religious law (Shari'a), thus giving Muslim culture a variety of external forms [Gibb, 1962a:3].

The significance of this factor is that the socio-cultural integration of the conquered peoples into the system of norms upheld by the dominant conquering group has not been problematic in the history of Islam. Neither has the Arab-Muslim conquest been associated in the conquered lands with the emergence of cleavages based on ethnic or class lines. Most of the countries invaded by the Arab-Muslims achieved the widest possible measure of social and cultural unity. This was reflected in the centrality of a common referent to which most segments of the population regardless of ethnic or class origins were committed. It was shared, in its nonreligious aspects, by many Christians and Jews who had not embraced Islam [Kirk, 1963:7].

One other important feature of the conquest was that the practices of female slavery and concubinage did not disrupt basic patterns of family organization in the conquered lands. Large-scale interbreeding between the conquerors and the women of different faiths played as important a part in the arabicization of the Middle East as it did in the iberianization of Latin America 800 years later. However, the Muslims did not for the most part enslave women from the conquered territories. Almost all male and female slaves were imported through the regular slave-market channels from Ethiopia, Central Africa, Anatolia, Spain, and Italy, which meant that the conquerors left indigenous family systems relatively intact [Levy, 1965:81-82]. No justifiable claim can be made that slavery and concubinage as practiced by the Muslims left all local women untouched. Some were undoubtedly

captured and treated as booty. However, by and large, one cannot
associate the Arab-Muslim conquest with the sexual exploitation
of local women or with the disintegration of the native family
systems of those lands which fell under their rule.

Islam: A Total Institution.--The second feature of Middle Eastern civilization, closely related to the first, stems
from the nature of Islam as an all-embracing normative system.
Basically, Islam is a religion designed to be a total institution,
a director toward higher values, and a normative guide for the
entire range of social behavior. There is a Muslim position on
nearly everything: war, citizenship, property, welfare, business,
crime, education, sexual intercourse, marriage, childbearing, and
divorce.

The view of the Quran (the Muslim holy book) as a divine
revelation regulating all facets of human existence had tremendous
repercussions on social institutions in the Muslim world. So
deep was the conviction that the public life of the Muslim community should rest upon the dicta of the Quran, as interpreted by
the jurists and reinforced by the exempla attributed to the prophet,
that the chief occupation of religious leaders came to be defin-
ing explicitly its pronouncements in the realms of ethics, norms,
and usages. This led to the production of the Shari'a (religious
law) which perpetuates religious norms for the entire range of
institutional activities: economic, political, legal, educational,
and familial [Gibb, 1948:186-189]. The effective precedents in
Shari'a law were drawn from the Quran and the Sunna (traditions)
of the prophet in his daily dealings. Local practices were legitimized and integrated into this all-embracing legal system by
either the consensus (ijam) of the legists or by a broad procedure of analogy (quiyas) to accepted Islamic practices.

Islam dominated all institutional structures throughout
the process of cultural amalgamation that characterized the Arab-
Muslim conquests, a dominance largely explained by the all-embracing nature of Islam which made no distinction between politics
and religion. However, the more effective and far-reaching integrative force in molding community life and in realizing the
social and cultural fusion of the conquered territories into a
common culture proved to be Shari'a law:

> By its very comprehensiveness it exerted a steady
> pressure upon all private and social activities,
> setting a standard to which they [the conquered]
> conformed more and more closely as time went on,
> in spite of the resistance of ancient habits and
> time honored customs. Islamic Law gave practical
> expression to the characteristic quest for unity.
> It went deeper than Roman Law. By reason of its

religous basis and its theocratic sanctions it was
the spiritual regulator, the conscience of the
Muslim community in all its parts and activities
[Gibb, 1962:10].

In contemporary Middle Eastern society the perpetuation
of Islam through the Shari'a as a potential agency of social
control has not gone completely unchallenged. However, for the
bulk of the Middle Eastern Muslim population, structures, attitudes, and practices derived from Islamic norms are maintained as
directive representations.

The indivisibility of religious doctrine from other aspects of community life has had two significant consequences for
social organization in the Middle East. First, it has established
a monolithic structure in which normative orientations to Islam
endow most aspects of society with religious significance, and
assign to each member a responsibility to relate these norms to
his major roles and social relationships. Under such conditions,
any institutional change tends to have religious implications.

Second, and in close conjunction, social organization
comes to be characterized by a unique type of institutional interdependency, binding specialized functional units together. The
possibility for an institution to achieve structural autonomy is
literally frozen [Bellah, 1958]. The family serves as a good
example for illustration because of its incapacity as a system
to become "differentiated" relative to the religious legal systems,
since religious law regulates all matters pertaining to the family.
The effect of this interdependency is to reinforce commitments to
the normative prescriptions governing family life, since any in-
fraction thereof would entail religious and legal sanctions.

The family system in the Middle East is the most salient
and central complex to reflect the extent of cultural fusion in
the Muslim-conquered lands. More than any other institution it
refdects the centrality of a common referent, a common normative
order to which all Muslims are deeply committed regardless of
nationality, ethnic background, or social class. In effect,
throughout the entire Middle Eastern complex the structure and
functioning of the family are practically identical, not only
among nomadic and settled peoples but also among the majority of
urban populations. Marriage customs, concepts of family honor,
sex mores, the position of the woman, and the division of labor
between the sexes are almost analogous everywhere in Muslim countries [Patai, 1955:1-21]. Those who have ventured outside the
narrow sphere circumscribed by Muslim tradition and inherited
custom comprise only a small minority of people among the urban
eduaated segment.

Shari'a law was particularly effective in regulating and unifying family behavior in the Muslim world during the conquest years when slavery and concubinage were widespread. By granting legal recognition to polygamy, slavery, and concubinage, religious law provided explicit provisions which placed slaves and concubines in definite positions within the kinship unit and the social structure and incorporated their offspring into the larger kinship group. Through this institutional support, slavery was prevented from becoming completely promiscuous and exploitative.

A cursory review of the legal and social stipulations regulating the relationship between a master and his female slave shows that slaves and concubines "belonged" to their owner, were subject to his control, and were granted the full protection of his household [Levy, 1965:78-82]. A slave could marry only with her owner's consent, but she could, of course, be sold or offered as a gift. However, any children she bore would always remain in her owner's household and under his protection.

Then again, it was common for the slave to become fully incorporated into her master's kinship unit. This was done either by her adoption, by her bearing his children, or by her becoming his legal wife. Once a slave bore her master's children, her position in the household was secure. She could not be resold or given away. In addition, her children would be free, if recognized by her master. In this case they would be entitled to the same legal privileges as those enjoyed by children of a legalized union. If the master did not recognize the children born of a slave, they would still remain in his household and under his protection. Upon the master's death, a slave who had borne children into the household would be freed, and so would all her children.

Obviously, there were variations in the institutional position between a legal wife, a concubine, and a slave, particularly with respect to rights of inheritance. Nevertheless, these differences were not pronounced insofar as the children were concerned. Islamic law places very few difficulties in the way of recognizing the legitimacy of children. Since both slavery and concubinage are theoretically lawful, it is not necessary for a mother to be married for her child to be declared legitimate. Even when a child is in danger of being born in doubtful circumstances some means or other is generally provided for in the law or in social custom to give it a show of legitimacy [Levy, 1965:135-139].

The effect of these explicit legal provisions upon the family was two-fold: they circumvented the incongruency of status that arises in a society where polygamy is unregulated and where numerous children are born under the stigma of illegitimacy, and they accelerated the integration of a "foreign" population into the socio-cultural system of the dominant group, thus buttressing the centrality of a common referent for family norms into which increasingly larger segments of the population were drawn.

The Absence of an Organized Clergy in Islam.--In Middle Eastern societies, tightly integrated and institutionally strong, control over women is delegated to and assumed exclusively by male members of the kinship group. No other institution has emerged to compete with male family members for a share in this control. Instead the prerogative of male members to impose restrictions on their women is supported by the entire institutional structure.

The supportive role of the judicial and religious systems in sustaining the primacy of kinship controls in the Middle East should not be underestimated. To a large extent their support is generated by the integrative aspect of Islam which negates explicitly or implicitly the structural autonomy of any one of these systems. However, it can be argued from a purely organizational point of view that the maintenance of kinship authority has also been facilitated by the absence of an organized clergy in Islam.

Drawing from the historical experience of the clergy in Europe and in Latin America, it is a known fact that religious organizations develop significant interests and obligations that can seriously conflict with family authority [Lorrimer, 1959:189-190; Blake, 1967:135]. With respect to Latin America it has been argued that religious elites generate their own organizational influence and organizational investments. The implication of such initiatives in modifying the systematic features of family control and in redefining the position of the woman in Latin America are just beginning to appear.

Middle Eastern societies, by contrast, operate under conditions where no conflict of interest exists between the religious and the family system. This allows Islam, as a religion, to fit in with a male authoritarian-centered family structure, to support it, in fact, instead of competing with it.

Would a conflict of interest between the clergy and the male population arise if an organized clergy were to emerge in the Middle East? It is doubtful. Islam has always enjoyed the strong involvement and political support of men because of the indivisibility of religious doctrine from political life and because of the legal precepts of the Shari'a which uphold a strong male-centered system of norms.

If Roman Catholicism has been described as nonfamilistic, Islam stands, if not in theory at least in practice, as antifeministic. The teachings of Muhammad may have emancipated the status of women in Arabia some 1,300 years ago. However, the major tendencies of Islamic law regarding the family and the institutional position of women were developed quite late in Islam, specifically during the height of the conquest period. As a result post-Quranic provisions became the effective precedents in Shari'a family law, and these tended to legitimize practices undermining inner family equality and solidarity and to elevate patriarchal arbitrariness [Bellah, 1968:16].

By the standards of the twentieth century, the religious sanctioning of polygamy and concubinage, divorce at will by the husband, guardianship of children to the father, unequal female inheritance, unequal weight to the legal testimony of women, are hardly consonant with a woman's equitable position in the modern world. It is not surprising that Islam as a religious system-- and in vivid contrast to Catholicism--has always had a much stronger hold over the male population than the female. Any voice that religious leaders would have concerning the structure of control over women would be to confirm and reinforce female sub- jugation to the authority of male members.

The mechanisms of social control in the two regions, al- though sharing some historical mutualities, clearly operate differ- entially as they relate to the institutional position of women in Latin America and the Middle East. Despite normative assertions to the contrary, there are marked differences between the socie- ties with respect to the extent to which social control systems are integrated and to the importance of the role assumed by the kinship unit in the structure of social control.

Chapter 7

THE SOCIAL CONTEXT OF WOMEN'S PARTICIPATION IN THE LABOR FORCE

The relationship is unmistakable between the differences in the structure of social control and the differences in women's participation rates in the nonagricultural labor force of Latin America and the Middle East. The imposition of social restrictions on women's personal imperative to work and the degree of assumption by the kinship unit of responsibility for the economic support of female relatives are expected to vary in direct proportion to the power of family control.

In Middle Eastern societies, where kinship is the basis of social organization, control is a tight monopoly of male family members undergirded by the full institutional support of the religious and judicial systems. Since control over women is legitimized in terms of family honor, the sanctions invoked against women working can be impenetrably prohibitive. However, for such sanctions to be fully effective, the kin group must assure uninterrupted economic support regardless of a woman's marital status. This is exactly what has happened in the Middle East up to now. The provisions made within the kinship structure are such that a male relative from the agnatic line is always economically, legally, and morally responsible for a woman regardless of her marital status. This means that the family is expected to extend economic support not only to female relatives who are single but to the widowed and divorced as well. Female participation in the nonagricultural labor force has remained low as a result both of the social stigma and of the assurance of economic support within the kinship structure. It is only when kinship liabilities for the economic support of female relatives begin to be questioned that the prerogatives of male members to censure their women are threatened.

In the Latin American situation, where the importance of family authority in the structure of social control has been challenged, normative standards of feminine behavior are not as easily enforced. Lower class males, stung by their inability to censure their women's conduct, are prone to feel little responsibility to support female relatives. In such cases women will work because of economic need. Among the privileged social classes, where kinsmen and clergymen compete for social control

101

over women, they have inadvertently provided alternative satisfactions and activities to women's traditional roles of marriage
and childbearing. Under such circumstances work participation
is not induced by economic need but comes as a result of women's
educational and occupational emancipation.

It is possible now to examine in greater detail the social
context in which women's work participation takes place in Latin
America and the Middle East to see whether the interpretation
advanced above holds true. In approaching the issue from this
perspective, several questions suggest themselves: What, if any,
are the resistances encountered by women who work? What is it
that is feared or threatening if women work? Who bears these fears
or threats, and what sort of relationship binds him with the
primary mover of these unpleasant feelings? What negative sanctions are applied to the working woman? What rewards are offered
to women who devote themselves to familial roles as opposed to
those who seek alternatives?

Because social control is expected to differ according to
marital status, and because the statistical presentation in Chapter 5 has already analyzed employment rates by marriage situation,
the positions of the nonmarried and the married women in the
social structure of Latin America and the Middle East are discussed separately.

The Single Woman

The pronounced differences in family characteristics between Latin American and Middle Eastern populations were shown
in Chapter 5. The most striking dissimilarities appeared in the
syndromes late-age-at-marriage/nonmarriage (typical of Latin
America) versus early-age-at-marriage/universality of marriage
(typical of the Middle East). Although the differences in marital-status structure were not tenable in themselves to account
for the regional differential in employment rates, further standardization analysis highlighted the substantive role of the single woman in the Latin American population in sustaining high
activity rates in that region. Two separate enquiries thus suggest themselves:

(a) Why are late marriage and nonmarriage more frequent
in Latin American societies than in the Middle East?

(b) How do marital delay and nonmarriage in Latin America
interact with the labor force?

In most societies marital delay and nonmarriage imply the
availability of opportunities for women to find satisfactions and activities alternative to marriage and childbearing. In the Latin

American countries the historical circumstances were of such magnitude as to make available to women a wider range of alternative behavior patterns from which to choose. These alternatives differ according to class: among the urban well-to-do, the Catholic clergy has contributed toward legitimizing women's educational and occupational emancipation by providing exclusive opportunities for higher education in racially and socially segregated climates, and by recruiting upper class women for semi-occupational functions. Being thus provided under the aegis of the Church with an identity outside of the circumscribed family roles, the middle and upper class woman in Latin American society has been able to overcome the social limitations of single status. Consequently, when marriage is delayed, or foregone altogether, there is little residue of an imposed penalty or shame.

Among the lower classes, women enjoy even greater latitude. Whereas Latin American women from the privileged strata may compensate for the lack of a husband by pursuing professional or religious careers, the lower class female is able to offset the disadvantage in many ways because of the wider range of alternative patterns of sexual behavior available to her. The result has been that a significant proportion of lower class women enter informal sexual unions, which are regarded as inferior to legal marriage but in which procreation takes place.

The structural conditions which have led to this situation were fully discussed in Chapter 6. There it was argued that marital patterns among the lower classes reflect the inability of family organizations to outgrow the legacy of the Spanish Conquest. Sexual exploitation of women prevails because family controls are inadequate to the task of enforcing sexual chastity or of pressuring a man to marry a girl whom he has made pregnant. Consequently, sanctions against illicit sexual relations, nonlegal marital unions, and birth-out-of-wedlock cannot be invoked effectively [Blake, 1962:89].

The absence of family controls--whether by choice or by necessity--has meant that courtship takes place without the supervision of an adult or adolescent peer. The situation that William Goode so aptly describes regarding courtship behavior in the Caribbean applies equally to Latin American society [1961: 910-925; 1960:21-30]. Unprotected by her kin, the girl has to establish an individual role bargain with the man. Since no conditions are set for their interaction, she has little chance of being married at all unless she is willing to accept a relationship outside of marriage. This often means risking childbirth as well. From the strictly motivational point of view, patterns of individual courtship outside of family controls have tended to render less effective the taboo on lost virginity. The pressure on a single girl to maintain her chastity is low because she gains very little either from her family or from the community

in the form of social rewards for settling down in marital poverty.
She may do better in an illegal union with a man of a higher
class than in a legal marriage with a man of her own rank. As
for the parents, it is inconsequential whether they succeed or
fail to align their daughter's behavior with the accepted norm.
Thus the formal sanction of a conjugal union fails to be fully
institutionalized; the prohibition against a nonlegalized union
fails to be fully sanctimonious. The result is that a large number of women are forced to substitute for marriage nonlegal living arrangements in the form of transient relationships of short
or ephemeral duration, consensual unions of some durability, and
polygamous concubinal unions with married men [Davis, 1964:37].

The prevalence of consensual unions, together with statistics on illegitimate births, provides a glaring indication of
the marginal influence exercised by the Catholic Church over the
masses. In theory consensual unions are condemned by the church;
in practice the local clergy have done little to enforce disapproval. Priests argue that they close their eyes to these practices for fear that any overt objection might alienate the lower
classes even further and drive them to abandon religious beliefs
altogether [Houtart and Pin, 1965:184].

Since most nonlegalized unions tend to be unstable, this
particular type of family structure has had a far-reaching impact
upon female employment rates. True, in certain rural areas consensual unions have proved to be stable and virtually indistin-
guishable from legalized unions. The same, however, cannot be
said of urban areas where the disruption of informal unions is
frequent [Arriaga, 1968:188; Stycos and Back, 1964:340]. Once a
consensual union is dissolved the woman finds herself in a position similar to that of the widow or the divorcee (particularly
if she has children), yet she has none of the rights and reci-
procities inherent in a legalized union. For civil and statistical purposes the woman reverts to a single status and her children are considered illegitimate. For structural purposes she is
left with a narrow range of expectancy punctuated by loosely
binding sexual relationships in all or most of which she will
bear children. However, until she is able to contract a new
union the woman is completely dependent upon herself for her own
and her children's economic survival. A situation is thus created which compels lower class women to work at intervals throughout their lives.

That the frailty of nonlegalized living arrangements in
Latin America thus operated as a powerful propellant thrusting
women into the work force is substantiated by the marital-specific activity rates, particularly when broken down according to
age and fertility status. For example, more than half of all
single women in Chile and more than 44 percent in urban Ecuador
ˋ employed. Moreover, their activity rates remain high through-

out their lifetimes. For example, in Chile more than 50 percent
of all single women between ages 20 and 49 are employed. Even
at more advanced ages, more than one-third remain in the labor
force. In urban Ecuador close to 60 percent of all single women
between ages 20 and 34 and approximately 50 percent between ages
35 and 59 are working. Even after age 60 the chances are that
one among every three single women is still working.

A further indication of the strong relationship between
unstable unions and high employment rates is provided by the
Chilean census which includes a cross-classification of women
workers by marital status and by number of live births. In that
country close to 15 percent of all single women have anywhere
from one to ten children. The employment activity rate of unwed
mothers is 44 percent, as compared to 24 percent among widowed
mothers, and 10 percent among married mothers.

Unstable consensual unions and illegitimate births do not
of course account for all the single women in the labor force.
Those who hold professional and white collar positions have presumably obtained them because of educational and occupational
emancipation. However, such cases are relatively rare. For example, less than 20 percent of all single female workers in Chile,
Costa Rica, and Peru are in upgraded occupations, compared to 50
percent who are in menial service jobs. It is the single woman
who supplies the bulk of labor in domestic household work. In
light of earlier suggestions, domestic work in particular can be
viewed as providing a convenient occupational outlet for women
in crisis situations which force them to seek work. Domestic
service does not require specialized training and does not involve long-term commitment or job continuity. At the same time
it provides anonymity since the girl is required to live at her
employer's home. For single women burdened with child care,
domestic service is perhaps the only income-earning activity
outside the home which allows them to keep their children with
them [Stycos and Weller, 1967:219].

In the Middle East the social position of the single
woman is antithetical. A social system where men have to safe-
guard continually against a woman's sexual misconduct or suspicion thereof necessitates a strong machinery of control geared to
secure the social insulation of the sexes and woman's nonexposure
to viable alternatives to marriage. Thus numerous and highly
effective institutional mechanisms preclude contact with the opposite sex. Some of the more significant indicators of the general seclusion patterns in Middle Eastern societies have been
mentioned in previous chapters: male/female segregation in most
public and private schools; parentally arranged nuptials; informal sex segregation in most recreational activities [Lacouture,
1958:406-409; Berger, 1964:99-100; Korson, 1969:155].

It is understandable, then, why there is a strong resistance in the Middle East to the employment of an unmarried girl. The position of the single woman in the social structure is, in fact, most precarious since any suspicion or mistrust of her moral conduct can stigmatize her and her family for life. However, the fact that the monopoly of social control is assumed by the kinship unit and is legitimized in terms of family honor explains only in part why so few single women work. Restrictive measures imposed upon single women by family and community controls are of course effective, yet female seclusion patterns could hardly have been sustained for long unless powerful mechanisms also motivated women's perception of a relationship between the social restrictions to which they are subject and their individual goals. Hence the need was not only to prevent women from seeking higher education or vocational training but also to withhold all inducements that would make a women want to seek employment in the first place.

Whereas in other societies an unmarried working girl enjoys economic independence, emancipation from parental control, and a more favorable bargaining position in the marriage market, in Middle Eastern countries she has none of these advantages. Her employed status does not liberate her from traditional family restraints. Working girls are not allowed to live on their own; they are granted neither freedom in their social life nor, in many cases, even the right to choose their own husbands. Except in the upper class, the earnings of a single woman are controlled by her parents. In some cases they are vital for the economic survival of the entire family. In addition, the mere fact that a girl works tends to jeopardize, rather than enhance, her chances of a good match. In the marriage market working girls are bound to be judged as loose, immoral and, in some cases, promiscuous, in contrast with girls who are secluded in their homes and are considered accordingly as paragons of virtue and chastity. Because female employment is linked with sexual misconduct, the working girl is under the continual scrutiny of her own family in every move she makes outside the home. Even employment of lower class single women in domestic service does not necessarily cancel out the principle of control because the servant girl exchanges not only households but also arbiters of her behavior. Her moral deportment reflects on the entire household of her employer. All in all, considering the strict control an unmarried girl is subjected to under paternal and fraternal authority patterns, it is clear why marriage becomes all the more attractive in view of the relatively greater freedom it affords.

Given the circumstances, it is not surprising that in Middle Eastern societies few single women work. In Turkey, Syria, and Egypt, among every 100 single women, only six, eight, and ten, respectively, are employed in nonagricultural pursuits, compared to an average of thirty-five in the Latin American countries.

Contrary to the situation in Latin America, however, among the working single women in the Middle East many are highly educated. For example, 42 percent of employed single women in Egypt and 35 percent in Syria hold professional and white collar jobs. The others are either in service occupations or in semi-skilled labor (Table 25).

Single women holding professional and white collar jobs represent the urban elite groups of Middle Eastern society and act as agents of modernization. Typically, in highly stratified societies, the behavior of such privileged social groups is spared much of the moral censure imposed on other segments. Hence, the fathers and brothers of these women are placed in a social position where they can afford to allow their women to work. However, it is important to note that the progressive attitude of this minority does not imply a general acceptance of permanent legitimate alternatives to marriage. In most Middle Eastern societies, modernity is a struggle to incorporate new patterns--in this case higher female education and occupational emancipation--within the traditional boundaries which define the female role in terms of marriage and motherhood [Carmelleri, 1967:594-596]. It is not an attempt to restructure relationships between the sexes in relation to society.

The Position of Women in Incomplete Families

The Widow.--The literature on family life in Latin America and the Middle East is not highly revealing on the subject of women who function in incomplete families, such as widows, divorcees, and those separated from their husbands. What little information is available, particularly when considered in conjunction with the labor force data, allows identification of certain differences in the institutional position of these women in the social structure of both regions.

It would appear that both societies make some provisions for the consequences of widowhood. The main difference is that in Latin America these obligations are not as explicitly spelled out by the kinship institutions nor are widows provided for economically to the same extent as they are in the Middle East.

There is little indication of the existence in Latin American family structure of specific prescriptions providing for the absorption of a widow into her own family unit or that of her late husband. Neither is there reference to explicit obligations incumbent upon male family members to provide for her support. The heavy migration of widows into urban areas suggests offhand that they must feel strong pressures to earn a living. The actual employment rates among this group, however, are too low to substantiate the claim that widows are in actuality

107

TABLE 25

WOMEN WORKERS DISTRIBUTED BY MARITAL STATUS, BY SPECIFIC
OCCUPATION, AND BY COUNTRY
(in percent)

Marital Status and Country	Occupation					
	Profes-sional	Admin./ Manag.& Clerical	Sales	Artisan, Crfstmen & Opera.	Ser-vices	Un-known
Single						
Chile	9.3	10.0	6.4	23.1	50.7	0.5
Costa Rica	13.5	9.4	8.7	15.7	52.1	0.6
Peru	6.9	8.9	7.2	16.0	56.7	4.3
Egypt	30.6	11.3	3.2	13.8	40.3	0.8
Syria	23.4	11.4	0.8	43.8	20.1	0.5
Divorced[a]						
Costa Rica	22.4	28.2	12.3	15.5	19.6	2.0
Peru	20.3	26.8	18.9	19.0	13.6	1.4
Egypt	6.4	3.4	15.5	13.4	61.0	0.3
Syria	17.0	3.0	4.2	39.5	36.3	---
Separated[b]						
Chile	10.2	15.0	11.1	25.3	38.2	0.2
Costa Rica	11.5	7.0	10.4	18.9	47.9	4.3
Peru	9.9	9.5	20.4	30.0	30.2	---
Widowed						
Chile	7.2	10.7	15.8	22.6	42.5	1.2
Costa Rica	10.3	9.3	12.7	18.7	45.8	3.2
Peru	5.4	6.5	28.2	32.5	25.4	2.0
Egypt	1.8	1.0	31.4	16.6	49.0	0.2
Syria	8.5	1.7	---	42.0	44.5	3.3
Married						
Chile	21.6	16.4	14.6	22.6	24.7	0.1
Costa Rica	42.7	13.1	9.6	16.2	16.9	1.5
Peru	19.2	10.7	22.3	31.5	14.7	1.6
Egypt	27.6	7.2	16.1	21.5	27.2	0.4
Syria	19.5	3.6	---	64.7	10.1	2.1
Consensual Unions[c]						
Chile	3.3	5.3	16.3	20.7	46.0	8.4
Costa Rica	4.9	5.3	13.0	23.6	48.9	4.3
Peru	1.8	2.4	24.4	34.5	33.0	3.9

[a]Divorce is not recognized in Chile.

[b]Separations are not recognized in the Middle East.

[c]Consensual unions are not recognized in the Middle East.

Sources: Chile, 1964:Table 20; Costa Rica, 1966:Table 37; Egypt, 1963:Table 20; Peru, 1964:Tables 101, 102; Syria, 1962: Table 42.

economically self-sufficient. In Chile, Costa Rica, and Peru, for example, an average of thirteen in 100 widows are employed in nonagricultural work. This ratio is very low when compared to the activity rates of the remaining nonmarried segment in the population, i.e. the single women and those who are divorced or separated from their husbands.

The general interpretation has been that Latin American widows migrate to urban areas because the village offers few employment opportunities. In light of their relatively low employment rates in nonagricultural activities, however, it is conceivable that their migration out of the village is prompted by social reasons as well. For a woman who has spent her entire life in the village, widowhood may well represent a chance to emancipate herself from rural ties. In the urban context the alternative means of support to the widowed group is most probably provided for by the extended family situation, whereby a married son or daughter who has already settled in the city would support a widowed mother.

Once a widow comes to an urban area, the probability of her remarriage is remote. One effect of the heavy migration of widowed women into the city is a considerable disparity in the ratio between unmarried males and females which is highly unfavorable for marital purposes. When, as is true of urban Chile, there are close to 250 potentially marriageable females between 35 and 55 for every 100 potentially marriageable males in the same age group, the chances for a widow to contract a sexual union, whether legal or otherwise, are scant. The interesting fact is that widows do not return to the rural areas where their chances for remarriage are five times higher than they are in urban centers. This can only mean that the social gains from urban life have outweighed whatever gains are offered by the village.

In Middle Eastern societies, the widowed woman is protected formally by explicit religious and legal prescriptions which stipulate that a Muslim woman always belongs to her kinship group. This originally tribal concept has several structural ramifications. It implies a set of institutional arrangements which hold kinsmen responsible for their female relative whatever her marital status. This is an unquestionable duty which in the eyes of many Muslim jurists was the justification of the bridal gift paid by the husband at the time of the marriage contract.

A widow's right to return with her children to her parental home is undisputed. Whether or not her family accepts her with enthusiasm, there are strong social pressures imposed upon the kin group to fulfill their duty toward the widowed daughter or sister. In societies such as the Middle East, where social control is largely based on shaming and depends on close groups in which everyone knows everyone else's business, the news that a widow is compelled to earn her own living would disparage or dishonor the male members of her family, for they would be liable to the accusation that they have exposed a helpless woman to the ignobility of the working world.

The kinship duty to support a widowed relative is an economic burden which most families are resigned to meet on a permanent basis since, in the Middle East, the remarriage of a widow is rare. Even the young widow typically has several children. This represents a deficit in the marriage market since expectations are great that the children will remain with their mother, a situation which is less probable for divorcees and may account, in part, for the divorcees' much higher remarriage rate. A widow's chances to remarry are further reduced by strong cultural superstitions in which she is labeled as a bad omen and associated with death [El Badry, 1956:22-34; Beck, 1957]. These factors combined provide sufficient rationalization to seclude the widow in her parental home where a life of chastity and continence dedicated to the memory of her late husband and devotion to her children are the only activities deemed proper for her to pursue.

In many Middle Eastern countries economic pressures are beginning to put to question the degree to which traditional family obligations should continue, yet the labor force data amply demonstrate that provisions for the economic support of widowed relatives are being acknowledged in actuality [Forget, 1962:117]. In fact, there is hardly any difference between the participation rates of married and widowed women. In Syria and in Turkey only 2 percent of widows are employed in nonagricultural occupations; in Egypt the corresponding figure is 3.5 percent. Compare these rates with those of Latin American countries where the propensity for widows to be employed averages six times higher than in the Middle East.

In both societies it is mainly the lower economic groups which supply widows to the labor force, as suggested by the specific occupations widowed women pursue. In all the countries under study widowed female workers concentrate heavily in artisan and service-type occupations. In Peru and in Egypt a substantial number of widows are also employed in petty trade. However, hardly any are in the upgraded occupations, such as the professions and white collar positions.

The Divorced Woman.--Since in Latin America legal marriage and consensual unions are the two ways in which a family unit is formed, it is important to distinguish marital disruption due to the dissolution of a consensual union from disruption due to legal divorce, separation, or annulment. Consensual unions are without legal status, thus, when they are dissolved the partners do not have the standard package of ties and obligations which inheres

among the divorced or the widowed. Women revert to the single
status and all children from such unions are considered illegitimate. The instability of consensual unions in urban areas creates
a structural situation which propels many single women and unwed
mothers into the nonagricultural labor force.

With respect to the dissolution of a legal marriage, the
situation differs only slightly. First, provisions for legal
divorce are not available in all Latin American countries. There
are, nevertheless, alternatives such as annulment (a costly under-
taking and hence an upper class privilege) and separation (typically the device of the poor). In the population as a whole, the
number of women classified as either divorced, separated, or marriage annulled, is minimal; which may be one reason why the literature on Latin American family life refrains from discussing their
position in the social structure.

The cross-classification of the labor force by marital
status indicates clearly that there must be strong pressures upon
Latin American women whose legal marriage has been disrupted by
reasons other than death to be economically self sufficient. In
all but Ecuador the employment rates among divorced/separated
women are the highest relative to all other marital groups. In
Peru close to 60 percent among this group are working in nonagricultural activities; in Chile 44 percent, and in Costa Rica 33
percent. The propensity is also high among this group to remain
in the labor force until advanced ages. In Chile 50 percent of
all divorced or separated women continue to work throughout the
age period 20 to 44. Between one-fourth and one-third are still
earning their living after they are 55 years old, which would
suggest that support from grown sons or daughters is not always
forthcoming.

It is interesting to note from the types of occupations
pursued by this group that there are distinct differences in
socio-economic background between the divorced and separated.
For example, in Costa Rica and Peru close to 50 percent of all
divorced female workers are in professional and white collar
employment, which denotes middle and upper social status. By
contrast, among the group who are separated those who work are
mostly employed in menial service jobs and in manual labor (Table
25).

Aside from certain factors, such as legal settlement,
which may place the divorcee in a more advantageous financial
situation, it is doubtful whether in Latin American society the
institutional position of the divorced or separated woman is in
any way different structurally from that of the single woman who
has left her nonlegal partner. The three statuses are equally
marginal and ambivalent in the social structure since institutional support is extended to none. These groups need to be

economically self-sufficient since the lack of institutional support is easily translated into lack of economic support as well. With respect to the forces in Latin American society which have resisted a legitimate definition of the status of divorced and separated women in the social structure, the influence of the Catholic Church can be traced along two directions. First, on the community level, the prohibition of the church has undoubtedly reinforced the social stigmatization of divorce and separation. Second, on a family level, the same prohibition has prevented the crystallization of any explicit post-divorce or post-separation arrangements within the family structure that could provide support for the female relative involved.

Women whose marriage has been annulled may not suffer from the same social stigma as the divorced or separated for two reasons. One, annulments are legitimized by the church, a sufficient reason for their social acceptance. Two, this quasi-divorce measure can be resorted to only by the upper classes because of the expense involved. The chances are that the upper class girl whose marriage has been annulled will be easily moved into a well-defined status within her family and her community. If she then decides to work it will be a voluntary decision on her part rather than one dictated by need.

In Middle Eastern society provisions for the consequences of divorce are particularly important to women because of the high frequency of legal dissolution and because the right to initiate such proceedings is a prerogative granted only to men. Hence, it is not surprising that Muslim kinship institutions prescribe the same set of moral and financial obligations toward divorced as toward widowed relatives. At the same time institutional arrangements provide the divorced woman with a well-defined status in the community while legal codes assign the responsibility of child care to the maternal grandparents until such time as the father claims his right of custody.

The structural position of divorced and widowed women in Middle Eastern society differs notably. Widows usually have children and seldom remarry. Divorcees typically are younger, are childless, and promptly remarry. Despite the high divorce rate, the proportion of adult women reported as currently divorced at any one time does not exceed 2 percent in most Middle Eastern countries [Goode, 1963:160-161; Lughod, 1965:242]. The one-third of divorcees who have children are relieved of a considerable portion of child-care responsibilities for Muslim law stipulates that children of divorced parents return to their father's care when the daughter is eleven and the son is nine. Until such a time, guardianship is legally assumed by either maternal or paternal grandparents. Religiously, divorce is a recognized institution; socially, the stigma against divorced women is imperceptible.

All these factors combined trigger a system of expectations by virtue of which the divorced woman is emboldened to compete with the single girl in the marriage market. This is how it happens. The divorced woman's situation is made to approximate as closely as possible that of the single girl. While virginity can no longer be offered as proof of moral conduct, evidence of continence can. Thus, to enhance the possibility of a good match, divorced women are often subjected to the same family restrictions and seclusion which are imposed upon single women. In exchange for these constraints the divorced woman is granted economic support and status placement within her family, both of which are necessary if remarriage is to be secured at a level which reflects favorably on her own standing.

This composite reflects traditional attitudes in Middle Eastern societies toward the divorced woman. More recently there is fragmented evidence that legal separation permits a wider latitude in the acknowledgment of kinship obligations and in the exercise of family authority. Whereas it has always been an indisputable duty of the Middle Eastern family to assume full financial responsibility for a widowed or divorced female relative, the recent view apparently promulgates that divorced women support themselves.

Judging from labor statistics alone it is no longer possible to substantiate the claim that kinship units provide economic support for divorced relatives to the same extent they do for the widowed. In Egypt, for example, the propensity for divorced women to be employed in the nonagricultural labor force is three times as high as it is for widows; in Syria it is four times as high; and in Turkey it is seven times as high. Furthermore, most of the employed divorcees work in service-type occupations, mainly as domestic help, which means that they may be geographically removed from male members of their household and thus placed at considerable distance from their supervision. Evidently then, family responsibilities and family controls are not as operative here as would have been expected.

A conceivable reason why divorced women, in particular, have been released from traditional restrictions is related to the high expectations that are initially placed upon their remarriage. Contrary to the widow, whose tragedy is a metaphysical one requiring a life of continence and seclusion, the divorced status is viewed as merely temporary. Once the divorced woman's situation is so defined, there are obvious repercussions when the initial expectations are not met. Given the high rate of remarriage among divorced women in most Middle Eastern countries, it follows that the divorcee who fails to contract a new union falls short of both societal and familial expectations. While the community may pity a family with a widowed daughter, the prolonged presence of a divorcee can become very embarrassing. Over the

113

years resentments against her may proliferate. Socially, she has failed her family by being unable to re-attract a marriage partner; economically she has become a continuing burden which was expected to be borne for only a limited period. Her failure could thus be rationalized by her family as sufficient justification for sending her to work. Not only does her default justify the family's action in their own eyes, but it also absolves them of much of the community censure which would have been expressed had the woman they sent away been only recently divorced.

This interpretation, if correct, would account for the high number of divorcees in the labor force as representing those who have been unsuccessful in finding husbands and consequently have been pressured into becoming economically self-sufficient. The decision to work is taken only when the hopes for eventual remarriage have been lost. Unfortunately, it is not possible to substantiate this explanation categorically because census statistics in the Middle Eastern countries fail to classify the labor force by age and by marital status simultaneously. Evidence in favor of this argument would be compelling, however, if an over-representation of divorced women appeared in the nonagricultural labor force at the older ages.

Of course, there are other possible explanations for the relatively high employment rate of divorced women in the Middle East. The heavy concentration of divorcees in urban centers may reflect not only the predominance of divorced women in internal migration, but also the higher frequency of legal dissolutions in towns and cities. This means that many of these women are far from their kin when their decrees are granted. The willingness of families to meet their obligations may be in inverse proportion to the physical distance involved. It is costly to bring a relative back home; it is even more costly to support her while she is in the city. Until her family is able to come to her assistance, a divorced woman has no alternative except to find work. Her decision to do so is apt to be an obvious economic relief to her family; her involvement is also easy to rationalize since distance obscures the fact that she works. Consequently, her employment will not have a drastic effect upon the family standing in the community.

Whatever explanation is accepted as accounting for the high work participation of divorced women in the Middle East, it is evident that legal separation permits a much wider latitude in the acknowledgment of kinship obligations. The current position of the divorcee is one indication of the incipient disintegration of traditional family obligations in the Middle East. Because of her youth, her right to forge a new life for herself, and her absolution from the need to prove her chastity, the divorcee becomes the most obvious target in the conflict between increasing economic pressures and the continued existence of

traditional obligations. The repercussions of such a conflict
upon the system of control are considerable, for once the family's economic responsibilities are weakened, the ability of male
members to impose restrictions and censure on their womenfolk
becomes nebulous.

The Married Woman in the Social Structure

In the Middle East the social position of the married
woman is similar in many respects to that of the middle and upper
class wife in Latin America. Strong pressures operate in both
regions to define the wife's role as explicitly subsidiary to
that of the husband. The paradigm of the wife is one of obedience
and seclusion; the husband's role stresses male superiority,
sexual bravado, and strong powers of social control. To the Middle Eastern wife this is hardly a surprise since it merely extends patriarchal authority. To the Latin American woman, however, marriage can represent a considerable loss of social freedom. Because in Latin America the major reference point of male
honor is the wife, social pressures restricting women's move-
ments and actions are directed more particularly at married women
[Wagley, 1968:73]. This explains why the normative patterns of
family life impose upon the wife a certain seclusion, relegate
her position to home-care and childbearing, and restrict her
social life to the company of close relatives and of members of
the clergy. By contrast, husbands in both Latin America and the
Middle East have a broader social life; their *amigo* system is an
accepted institution; and so are their extra-marital affairs. In
short, a separate male and female ethos is striking in both societies.

What has just been said does not apply to marital relationships among the lower classes in Latin America, nor to consensual unions. In both these cases different sex norms and concepts
of the male role prevail. Lower class women are not circumscribed
by the explicit rules upheld by the privileged classes. Consequently, virginity is not a prerequisite for marriage; there is
no perceptible discrimination between the sexually experienced
woman and one who has had no affairs; segregation of the sexes is
relaxed; marital infidelity is common; and marriages are quite
unstable [Adams, 1967:154; Azevedo, 1965:296].

Middle Eastern wives are far more subjugated than even the
most rigidly circumscribed of upper class Latin American wives
because of the institutional complex in Middle Eastern society
which re-affirms the subordinate position of the married woman.
In all Middle Eastern countries except Turkey and Tunisia, marriage norms are derived from Islamic law and incorporated in
letter and spirit into the Personal Statute Codes. By virtue of
their religious origin these laws are hallowed by divine sanction

and are resistant to secular attempts at modification. Muslim law grants males the prerogatives of divorce, polygamy, guardianship over children, and the enforcement of the return of a rebellious wife to the conjugal home. Obviously not all Muslim men take advantage of these privileges. Nevertheless the mere fact of their legal endorsement functions as a constant and concrete source of anxiety to many married women.

Latin American societies, by contrast, contain sufficient legal provisions and institutional support to ensure the continuity of a legitimate family. Although institutional arrangements in those societies cannot guarantee a faithful husband, the prohibition of legalized polygamy and the restrictions on divorce guarantee to the married woman a certain sense of security. The fact that in the legal systems of the Latin American countries equal rights of inheritance are guaranteed to both sexes affords an additional advantage to the Latin American wife that her Middle Eastern counterpart does not enjoy. Although Muslim law grants women independent control of their property, males are assigned twice as much property as females.

One important difference between the position of married women in Latin America and the Middle East was discussed in an earlier chapter. There it was argued that in Middle Eastern societies no formal influence outside of the kinship unit has emerged to challenge the authority of the husband, whereas in Latin America control over the middle and upper class married woman is shared between the husband and the priest. Other than her own relatives, the only ally a Latin American wife can count upon is the church. The Spanish Catholic clergy have helped to promulgate such an alliance because it reflects favorably on their interests. Thus instead of attempting to rectify the double standard characterizing marital relationships among the upper social groups, the clergy has persisted in preaching an acquiescent attitude toward male prerogatives and stressing woman's moral responsibility to maintain the integrity of the family. The benefits derived by the clergy from the shifting balance of power are considerable, for as more married women turn to religion for comfort, they fall increasingly under the influence and control of the church.

Some married women in Latin America are undoubtedly content to seek in religious doctrines the consolation of laudable self-sacrifice and the prospect of heavenly protection. Others, however, perceive in the increasing influence of the clergy a means to emancipate themselves, albeit partially, from the authority of their husbands. By playing these two forces against each other, some married women in Latin America are able to dilute institutional control and evolve for themselves a role and identity outside of both family and church.

Societal Reaction to the Working Wife

There is strong resentment in both Latin America and the Middle East to the independent employment of married women. The traditional conception in Latin America has been that when married women work, the role of the man as protector and head of the household is weakened. A woman who earns money outside the home and is identified as working in the proximity of men is viewed as an insult to and a breach of the sanctity of the home. Such ideals are not necessarily held by lower class families where more often than not the wife supports the entire household.

The position against the employment of married women, in general, is supported both by the church and by the legal system. The Catholic Church has taken a strong line against working wives, with Pope Pius XII commenting that "It is a corruption of women's nature and motherly dignity and disruption to the whole family. By working outside the home the woman will relapse into her former servitude and as in pagan times she will become the instrument of man." Legal institutions in some Latin American countries grant judicial authorities the right to prohibit a married woman from working if her husband objects to it. In Chile the weighting is so unequal that a husband is not required to offer any evidence that his working wife is neglecting her home. He need not justify his refusal for her to continue working. It is enough that he refuses.

Resentment against the participation of married women in the labor force is most intense in the Middle East. In those societies the most frequent criticism leveled against working wives revolves around the so-called dangers of promiscuity. Many Middle Eastern men view work as a locus providing free access for women "to play around with men." Educated Moroccan men openly admitted to a lack of confidence in married women, whom they considered in need of protection against their own weaknesses. This may be an extrapolation to the wives of other men of their feelings about their own wives. In a survey conducted in Rabat, Moroccan men explained their persistent mistrust of women as a result of the arranged-marriage system, where family pressure often prevails over the will of either spouse. In the men's own words: "There is no reason for having confidence in a woman whom you know has married you in obedience to her parents wishes, or because there was nothing else for her to do" [Forget, 1962:107]. It takes a strongly motivated woman to counteract such deeply entrenched biases.

Even among Middle Easterners holding liberal views about the right of married women to work, appropriate jobs are circumscribed. Women must have few contacts with a male public and outsiders must not see women interacting with men. The medical

117

and teaching professions are particularly favored because women in these occupations are in contact only with other women and with children.

The marital-specific employment rates shown in Table 16 indicate clearly that the norm for married women not to work is upheld, in varying degrees, both in Latin American and Middle Eastern societies. In Chile, Costa Rica, Ecuador, and Peru, an average of only eight in 100 married women are working in non-agricultural activities. Even women living in informal unions seem to adhere to normative expectations ascribed to the legally married. Except for Chile, where consensual mates display a slightly higher propensity to work than the legally married, the employment rates for both statuses are almost identical.

In Middle Eastern society married women are virtually absent from the nonagricultural labor force: typically, one percent in the total population and 6 percent in the urban work force. On average, six times as many married women work in Latin America as in the Middle East, although this difference is reduced considerably in the urban setting. For example, the employment rate of married women in urban Ecuador is less than three times the corresponding rate for women in Turkey.

Given the difference in normative expectations between the lower and upper social groups in Latin America concerning the behavior prescribed for the married woman, one would expect working wives to be essentially a lower class phenomenon. Table 25, which classifies the occupational distribution of women workers by marital status, shows that this is not so. A substantial percentage among the working wives belong to the privileged classes. For example, in Costa Rica close to 43 percent of all the married women employed in nonagricultural activities are in the professions; in Peru and Chile between 30 and 38 percent are in the professions and in white collar employment. These occupations require the kind of training that is attained almost exclusively by the middle and upper social strata. In this connection the impetus supplied by the Catholic Church in providing occupational opportunities for upper class women and in creating a structural situation allowing some married women to evolve for themselves a nontraditional role should not be underestimated.

The Egyptian figures also indicate a considerable number of highly educated women among the working wives. For example, close to 30 percent of all the married female workers hold professional jobs and 7 percent are in white collar employment.

The possibility for higher educational qualifications to surmount barriers against the employment of married women in traditional societies has been noted in other countries. It appears to be equally true of Latin American and Middle Eastern

societies that married men from the more privileged social strata
can more easily overcome their scruples about working wives if
the women have sufficient education to obtain a prestigious position [Carleton, 1965:233-234]. Within the limited range of available professions, most women indicate a preference for teaching.
Since almost all schools are sex-segregated at post-primary levels,
Middle Eastern husbands are guaranteed professional careers for
their wives in conservative surroundings where opportunities for
contact with the opposite sex are minuscule.

Chapter 8

CONCLUSION

Two primary objectives guided this study. The first aim
was to analyze, on the basis of data available, comparative differences in the extent to which women in developing countries
participate in economic activities other than agriculture. The
second purpose, which constituted the major portion of the research, was to interpret the striking differentials in female
employment rates between two regions currently in the process of
industrialization: Latin America and the Middle East.

In terms of quantitative comparative data, countries in
the two regions are at roughly similar stages of economic development. However, whereas the Latin American countries report
the highest female employment rates in nonagricultural activities
among all developing nations, the Middle Eastern region systematically reports the lowest female participation rates on record.
The Middle Eastern behavior deviates from the current experience
of other developing nations and also from the historical experience of the now-industrialized West. The sociological task of
this study was directed toward uncovering the correlates of female labor force participation in nonagricultural work and the
extent to which these correlates differ between Latin American
and Middle Eastern societies.

An explanation for the regional differential was sought
first in an analysis of factors governing labor demand through
a detailed examination of the industrial and occupational structure
of the nonagricultural labor force. The thirteen countries in
this study proved to be generally similar in the specific organization of their nonagricultural economies despite some marked
dissimilarities in employment of women therein. Evidence of the
negative influence of factors related first to the level of
economic development and second to the structure of demand for
workers pointed to the limitation of invoking economic variables
to explain the regional differential in women's involvement in
the work force. In this respect, the evidence presented indicated clearly the inconsistency with which the female labor force
reacts to economic development levels and to work opportunities
available in the labor market.

CONCLUSION

An investigation of two main factors controlling the
supply of female labor independently of demand divulged considerable differences between Latin American and Middle Eastern
societies. First, the comparative regional differences in female educational attainments highlighted the low educational
standards of Middle Eastern women. At the same time, evidence
of the accelerating effect of higher education upon female employment rates in the Middle Eastern countries underlined the role
of educational deprivation in depressing women's employment rates
in that region. The hypothetical effect of providing Turkish and
Egyptian women with the same educational standards prevailing in
Chile and Colombia was tested. The results projected more than
a twofold increase in the female employment rates in the two Middle Eastern countries.

Second, the relative importance of marital and fertility
characteristics upon female employment rates was investigated in
an attempt to explain the regional differential in feminine labor
force behavior. In all the Middle Eastern countries the characteristics of the female population did not favor woman's availability to the labor market, whereas in Latin America they appeared
to be highly conducive to a large-scale participation. Despite
the striking differentials between the two female populations
with respect to variables centrally related to women's employability, evidence of the influence of these differences upon the
female employment rates was insufficient. When the female population in Latin America was subjected through standardization
analysis to the family conditions of women in the Middle East,
they continued to manifest high overall activity rates. An estimation of the womanpower potential that exists in the Middle
Eastern societies, given their actual family characteristics,
showed that if Middle Eastern women had the same propensity to
work within each specific age-group by marriage class as women
had in Latin American countries, a fivefold increase in the female activity rates of Middle Eastern countries could be effected.

These findings suggested that the supply of women available to the labor market was not merely a function of family
characteristics such as age-at-marriage, extent of marriage, prevalence of marital disruption, and fertility rates. Rather, it
was the interaction of such variables with the social organization that determined the contribution of women to nonagricultural
economic activities. The results obtained from standardization
procedures indicated convincingly that in the Middle Eastern
countries the constraints imposed upon women's imperative to work
were not related to their wife-mother role. In those societies
female employment rates were low because all women were restricted,
regardless of age, marital condition, or motherhood state.

The search for an explanation of the regional differential was thus pressed through major aspects of social organization

and their cultural adjuncts. The features receiving special emphasis were the cultural definition of the female role, the role of the kinship unit in the system of social control, and the acknowledgment of economic obligations to female family members as prescribed by kinship institutions in Middle Eastern and Latin American societies.

Answers to some of the questions raised regarding possible differences in the ideal patterns of feminine behavior, the institutional context of kinship organization, and the machinery of social control over women between the two societies could not be found in the "normative" framework of Latin American and Middle Eastern social organizations. Both societies were found to be characterized, normatively, by a traditional social order noted for its strong familism, patriarchialism, cultural tradition of male supremacy, and the positive sanctioning of religion (Catholicism in one and Islam in the other) which reinforced the subordinate position of the woman in the social structure. Given this common context, it was necessary to pursue our query further into particular elements of the social structure in Latin America and the Middle East in order to uncover how, in actuality, the machinery of social control operated in each society and what impact it exercised upon the institutional position of the women.

Two distinctive features exceptional to Latin America were singled out for discussion because of the decisive roles they played in weakening the monolithic system of family authority over women and concomitantly thwarting the institutionalization of certain normative patterns of family life. First was the historical factor of the Spanish conquest which widened ethnic and class differences and made extremely difficult the social and cultural integration of the indigenous population into the system of norms upheld by the dominant social group. Second was the powerful influence exercised by the highly organized and putatively celibate Catholic clergy over women from the privileged strata.

Even if all Latin Americans were to participate in the same system of cultural values, family life would still present itself to the individual in a different structural context according to his location in the social structure. Among the lower classes male members have not outgrown the Spanish legacy of concubinage. As a result there is considerable collapse in control functions of kinsmen over their womenfolk. Among the privileged groups, control over women is shared between clergy and kinsmen. The close association of the Latin American women with the church meant that priests succeeded in evolving a competitive role for themselves vis-à-vis male members of the family group and thus prevented males of the family from completely dominating the existential behavior of their women. Both factors have been part of the challenge to the characteristic system of family control and have resulted in noteworthy behavioral adaptations among family members, in general, and women, in particular.

122

CONCLUSION

The behavioral adjustments of women have ranged anywhere from sexual promiscuity to professional emancipation. Of critical importance here is that situational circumstances have created a wider range of alternative patterns of behavior for women to supplement the single traditional role ascribed by culture and sustained by family ideals. The fact that so many Latin American women took advantage of these alternatives explains the inconsistency and contradiction between the cultural definition of the female role and the actual feminine behavior in Latin America.

This situation contrasts sharply with the Middle Eastern institutional structure which depends entirely upon kinship and the family as a basis of social organization. Kinship institutions presuppose the constant presence of a male member who is economically, legally, and morally responsible for the woman, whatever her marital status. This is true for all social classes. The monopoly of control over women is thus tightly integrated. Control is delegated to and assumed exclusively by male members of the kinship group with the full institutional support of the religious and the judicial systems.

The relationship between these different structures of control and women's participation in the labor force is considerable because kinship acknowledgments of economic responsibilities to female members vary in direct proportion to the power of social control vested in the family unit. Where family control over women collapses, women are forced to be self-sufficient at numerous intervals in their lives because of the weak commitment of males to acknowledge economic responsibilities. Where social control is shared between two competing groups, women can play one authority against the other and take advantage of the alternatives available. Work participation will be high in this case because of educational and occupational emancipation. Where social control is monopolized by one strong network, and where seclusion is legitimized in terms of family honor, the sanctions invoked against women working can be mighty. However, for such sanctions to be fully effective it becomes incumbent upon the kinship unit to provide economic support for their women at all times. This is exaxtly what has occurred in the Middle East. In those societies few women work because of the combined effects of social stigmatization and the provision of economic support within the kinship structure. It is only when family responsibilities for the economic support of female relatives begin to be questioned, as they are being questioned concerning the divorced woman in the Middle East today, that the prerogatives of male members to impose restrictions on women stand on shaky grounds.

Theoretical Considerations

The results of this study are definite on two points of theoretical importance. First, despite the experience of the industrialized West, the introduction of mechanical industries into a previously nonindustrialized society does not automatically foster a trend toward women's increased participation in nonagricultural economic activities. Our findings constitute compelling evidence to the effect that economic development does not affect behavior except in terms of social organization. The starting social and cultural systems differ among societies, and in the initial stages of industrialization there may well be differences in the response of a marginal element such as the female labor force.

Second, regarding the importance of family organization as a patterning implement of women's participation in the labor force, we hope we have made it evident that no one distinctive institutional arrangement conduces to a large-scale work involvement of women. The examples of Western Europe during its early phase of industrialization and of Latin America today serve to illustrate this argument. In both societies the propelling factor in the growth of the female labor force came in the form of an influx of single women into the labor market. However, the causal elements for the availability of this supply differ between the two societies: in the West the supply emanated from altered social and economic conditions which helped to emancipate women and to redefine their role and status in society. In Latin American countries the supply of available women is related to family disorganization, to the prevalence of nonlegalized sexual unions, and to high rates of illegitimate births, all of which give rise to situations where single women are compelled by economic need to seek work at numerous intervals in their lives.

One major feature links the West and the Latin American societies and makes their situation different from that of the Middle East. In the linked regions the structural independence of the nuclear family from a ramified kinship system has been bolstered by a strong religious organization which is highly competitive with the family for loyalty toward personnel and property. The influence of the Catholic Church upon the role of women, in general, and upon their participation in the work force, in particular, has been striking. It explains, in large part, why the position of the Latin American woman is closer to the Western pattern than it is to that of the Middle East, despite normative assertions to the contrary.

Future Influences on Labor Participation

In the Middle East there are many hindrances to the increase in the number of women in the nonagricultural labor force, but several manipulable variables may speed greater participation. One is the economic factor. That the actual participation of Middle Eastern women in the labor force is drastically below what might be expected means that the social gains of not working have so far outweighed the economic gains.

Nevertheless, recent changes in most Middle Eastern countries have increased economic pressures so greatly that it is becoming difficult for men to continue to meet their kinship obligations toward their womenfolk. Such constraints have already begun to be felt with respect to divorced sisters and daughters. Continued pressure in this direction will lead the single woman to enter the labor market. Weakened family economic relationships will be the nemesis of male prerogatives to restrict and censure women.

The function of the second manipulable variable--higher education--must be neither minimized nor exaggerated. It is important because it has fostered aspirations and attitudes among women in the Middle East which increase their participation, as evidenced by the accelerating effect of educational levels upon women's labor force rates. A long period of education serves to postpone marriage, to increase areas of aspiration, presumably to instigate a rational and secular point of view, and to make possible participation in society at a higher status. A continued rise in education, however, cannot be guaranteed to sustain high participation rates unless the economic system develops as education increases and affords additional occupational opportunities.

Economic pressures and increased education are major catalysts in speeding the labor force participation of women in Latin America. They are expected to have the same effect in the Middle East. However, a cautionary reservation seems in line here.

The extent to which women will be motivated to work will ultimately depend on the degree to which changing social conditions bring acceptance and recognition of women's worth for the contributions they can make outside of traditional family roles. To effect a change in social attitudes toward women's work is somewhat different from the prevalence of conditions which *force* women into the labor market because of economic need. In the long run the one may affect the other. From the motivational point of view, the sum total of conditions must be so balanced as to elicit the perception of a relationship between woman's participation and individual goals. The social setting must be such as to reward women's efforts to participate in the work force in forms other than financial remuneration and intellectual satisfaction. More important, the social order has to allow for the integration of woman's economic role within its system of rewards. This is in large part what we have in mind when we state that the social organization must itself be modified to allow women legitimate alternatives and satisfactions outside of the family roles.

INDUSTRIAL WORKERS IN MEXICO AND EGYPT: DISTRIBUTION BY
TYPE OF INDUSTRY AND BY FEMALE PERCENTAGE
(Population 15+)

Type of Industry and Occupational Group	MEXICO			EGYPT		
	Total	Female	Percent Female	Total	Female	Percent Female
Public and Administrative Services						
Professional	280,304	130,776	44.6	186,752	47,023	25.2
Managerial	27,943	3,053	10.9	682,582	2,061	0.3
Clerical	331,293	108,395	32.7	143,311	4,458	3.1
Sales	56,168	17,391	30.9	6,396	235	3.7
Operatives	65,958	18,990	28.8	245,439	18,015	7.3
Service	25,874	11,014	42.5	451,044	5,582	1.2
Commerce						
Professional	22,359	5,846	26.1	4,696	215	4.6
Managerial	25,505	6,085	23.8	7,344	186	2.5
Clerical	103,515	29,790	28.7	35,522	3,523	9.9
Sales	875,806	242,005	27.6	533,982	30,133	5.6
Operatives	37,829	3,152	8.3	18,924	642	3.4
Service	9,578	3,459	36.1	8,064	72	0.9
Transport						
Professional	6,523	978	14.9	4,713	110	2.3
Managerial	3,463	213	6.2	4,872	93	1.9
Clerical	63,194	11,199	17.7	20,606	1,051	5.1
Sales	3,552	550	15.5	554	5	0.9
Operatives	274,042	3,448	1.3	289,146	828	0.4
Service	5,282	1,467	27.8	11,445	156	1.4
Manufacturing						
Professional	46,968	8,388	17.8	8,338	228	2.7
Admn./Clerical	135,336	29,727	21.9	34,596	1,539	4.4
Sales	53,399	12,835	24.4	4,942	137	2.7
Operatives	1,296,662	182,912	14.1	607,607	18,980	3.1
Service	24,990	15,778	63.1	11,976	173	1.4
Extractive						
Professional	11,785	2,186	18.5	809	18	2.2
Admn./Clerical	16,974	3,359	19.7	1,166	43	3.6
Sales	2,109	397	18.8	53	1	---
Operatives	109,026	3,122	2.8	17,364	19	0.1
Service	1,907	538	28.2	852	3	0.3
Electricity and Gas						
Professional	3,557	426	11.9	1,218	13	1.0
Admn./Clerical	13,677	2,408	16.6	3,690	144	3.9
Sales	1,172	192	16.3	9	---	---
Operatives	22,313	626	2.8	29,230	76	0.2
Service	726	249	34.2	1,377	15	1.0
Construction						
Professional	18,237	1,984	10.8	2,693	6	---
Admn./Clerical	17,694	1,765	9.9	8,928	66	0.7
Sales	1,840	268	14.5	615	1	---
Operatives	386,768	7,998	2.1	141,013	344	0.2
Service	3,863	2,146	55.5	1,519	12	0.7
Domestic Svc.	721,269	483,250	67.0	114,383	73,606	64.4

Sources: Mexican data compiled from Direccion de Estadistica y
Censos [1964], Table 22; Egyptian data from Department
of Statistics and Census [1963], Table 28.

APPENDIX TABLE 2

MIDDLE EASTERN INDUSTRY WORKERS: PERCENTAGE DISTRIBUTION
BY EMPLOYMENT STATUS AND SEX
(c.1960)

Country	Total Workers (100 percent)		Employment Status							
			Salaried/ Wage Earners		Employers/ Own Account		Family Workers		Status Unknown	
	M	F	M	F	M	F	M	F	M	F
Egypt	679,753	24,526	79.4	61.0	16.7	22.9	3.7	16.0	0.1	0.0
Iran	758,799	508,801	71.6	51.6	26.1	29.8	2.1	19.1	0.2	0.2
Libya	21,464	7,913	59.7	7.8	23.5	22.5	3.0	67.8	1.1	0.0
Morocco	186,042	80,261	59.2	38.2	37.3	53.6	2.4	4.2	1.1	4.2
Pakistan	2,195,540	258,646	35.8	5.9	56.9	63.4	7.3	30.6	---	---
Syria	109,374	8,026	74.3	73.0	22.4	15.1	3.3	11.9	---	---

Source: International Labor Office [1970], Table 2.

SELECTED BIBLIOGRAPHY

Adams, R. 1967. *The Second Sowing: Power and Secondary Development in Latin America*. San Francisco: Chandler.

_____, et al. 1960. *Social Change in Latin America Today*. New York: Random House.

Andreski, S. 1969. *Parasitism and Subversion: The Case of Latin America*. New York: Schoken.

Arriaga, E. 1968. Some Aspects of Family Composition in Venezuela. *Eugenics Quarterly* 15.

Axelrod, M., Goldberg, D., and Slesinger, D. 1963. Current Fertility Expectations of Married Couples in the United States. *Population Index* 29.

Azevedo, T. de. 1965. Family, Marriage and Divorce in Brazil. In *Contemporary Cultures and Societies of Latin America*, ed. R. Adams. New York: Random House.

Bancroft, G. 1958. *The American Labor Force: Its Growth and Changing Composition*. New York: Wiley.

Beck, D. 1957. Changes in the Muslim Family in the Middle East. *Journal of Marriage and Family Living* 19(4).

Bellah, R. 1958. Religious Aspects of Modernization. *American Journal of Sociology* 64.

_____. 1968. Islamic Tradition and the Problem of Modernization (mimeo).

Berger, M. 1962. *The Arab World*. New York: Doubleday.

_____. 1964. *The Arab World Today*. New York: Doubleday.

Blachere, R. Regards Sur l'Acculturation des Arabes Musulmanes Jusqu'à Vers 40/661. *Arabica* 3.

Blake, J. 1962. *Family Structure in Jamaica*. New York: Free Press.

_____. 1965. Demographic Science and the Redirection of Population Policy. *Journal of Chronic Diseases* 18.

_____. 1967. Parental Control, Delayed Marriage and Population Policy. *Proceedings of the World Population Conference, 1965*. Vol. II, United Nations.

Blitz, R. 1964. The Chilean Educational System and its Relation to Economic Growth. In *Education and Economic Development*, ed. A. Anderson and M. J. Bowman. Chicago: Aldine.

Boktor, A. 1963. *School and Society in the Nile Valley*. Cairo: American University at Cairo.

Carleton, R. 1965. Labor Force Participation: A Stimulus to Fertility in Puerto Rico. *Demography* 2.

Carmelleri, C. 1967. Modernity and the Family in Tunisia. *Journal of Marriage and Family Living* 29.

Chile. 1964. Dirección de Estadística y Censos, XIII Censo de Población 1960. *Características Basicas de la Población.* Santiago.

Código Civil de la República de Chile. Artículos 150, 1954; *Código Civil de la República de los Estados Unidos Mexicanos*. Artículo 170.

Collver, H., and Langlois, E. 1962. The Female Labor Force in Metropolitan Areas: An International Comparison. *Economic Development and Cultural Change* 10(4).

Colombia. 1967. Departmento Administrativo Nacional de Estadística, *XIII Censo Nacional de Población*. Bogota.

Costa Rica. 1966. Dirección General de Estadística y Censos, *1963 Censo de Población*. San Jose.

Daghestani, K. 1932. *Étude Sociologique Sur la Famille Musulmane Contemporaine en Syrie*. Paris: Leroux.

D'Antonio, W., and Pike, F. 1964. *Religion, Revolution and Reform*. New York: Praeger.

Daric, J. 1958. Quelques Vues Sur le Travail Femenine Non-Agricole en Divers Pays. *Population* 13.

Davis, K. 1954. Urbanization and the Development of Pre-Industrial Areas. *Economic Development and Cultural Change,* Vol. 3.

_____. 1964. The Place of Latin America in World Demographic History. *Milbank Memorial Fund Quarterly* 14(2).

_____. 1967. Population Policy: Will Current Programs Succeed? *Science* 158.

_____. 1969. *World Urbanization 1950-1970.* Vol. I. *Basic Data for Cities, Countries and Regions.* Berkeley: University of California, Population Monograph Series #4.

_____. 1972. *World Urbanization 1950-1970.* Vol. II. *Analysis of Trends, Relationships and Development.* Berkeley: University of California, Population Monograph Series #9.

de Hoyos, A., and de Hoyos, G. 1966. The Amigo System and Alienation of the Wife in the Conjugal Mexican Family. In *Kinship and Family Organization,* ed. B. Farber. London: Wiley.

Ecuador. 1964. División de Estadistica y Censos. *Caracteristicas de la Población y Vivienda del Ecuador* (Preliminary results 3% Sample of National Census Returns taken 25 November 1962). Quito.

Egypt. 1963. Department of Statistics and Census. *General Census of Population 1960,* Vol. II. *General Tables.* Cairo.

el Badry, M. 1956. Some Aspects of Fertility in Egypt. *Milbank Memorial Fund Quarterly* 34.

Forget, Nelly. 1962. Attitudes Towards Work by Women in Morocco. *International Social Service Journal* 14.

Foster, P. 1964. The Vocational School Fallacy in Developmental Planning. In *Education and Economic Development,* ed. A. Anderson and M. J. Bowman. Chicago: Aldine.

Freedman, R., Whelpton, P. K., and Campbell, A. A. *Family Planning, Sterility and Population Growth.* New York: McGraw Hill.

Freedman, R., Baumart, G., and Bolte, M. 1959/1960. Expected Family Size and Family Values in West Germany. *Population Studies* 13.

Futuh, Abu Al, A. 1951. *Old and New Forces in Egyptian Education.* New York: Columbia University.

Gendell, M. 1965. The Influence of Family Building Activities on Women's Rate of Economic Activity. *World Population Conference* 2.

Gibb, H. A. R. 1948. The Structure of Religious Thought in Islam. *Muslim World* 38(3).

_____. 1962a. *Studies on Civilization of Islam.* Boston: Beacon.

_____. 1962b. *Mohammedanism: A Historical Survey.* New York: Galaxy.

Goode, W. 1960. A Deviant Case: Illegitimacy in the Caribbean. *American Sociological Review* 25.

_____. 1961. Illegitimacy, Anomie and Cultural Penetration. *American Sociological Review* 26.

_____. 1963. *World Revolution in Family Patterns.* Glencoe: Free Press.

_____. 1971. Family Disorganization. In *Contemporary Social Problems,* ed. R. Nisbet. New York: Harcourt Brace Jovanovich.

Grabill, W. J., Kiser, C., and Whelpton, P. 1958. *The Fertility of American Women.* New York: Wiley.

Gutierrez de Pineda, V. 1964. *La Familia y Cultura en Colombia.* Bogotá: Universidad Nacional de Colombia.

Hamady, S. 1960. *Character and Temperament of the Arabs.* New York: Twayne.

Hammel, E. A. 1961. The Family Cycle in Coastal Peruvian Slum and Village. *American Anthropologist* 63.

Hanke, L. 1968. *Contemporary Latin America: A Short History.* New York: Van Nostrand.

Harbison, F., and Myers, C. 1964. *Education, Manpower and Economic Growth.* New York: McGraw Hill Series in International Development.

Hartley, S. 1969. Comparative Differences and Changes in Levels of Illegitimacy. Unpublished Ph.D. dissertation, University of California, Berkeley.

Heer, D. 1964. Fertility Differences Between Indian and Spanish-speaking Parts of the Andean Countries. *Population Studies* 18(1).

132

_____. 1965. Economic Development and Fertility. *Demography* 3.

_____, and Turner, E. 1965. Areal Differences in Latin American Fertility. *Population Studies* 18(3).

Heller, P. B. 1963. Demographic Aspects of Development in Contemporary Egypt. Unpublished Ph.D. dissertation, New York University.

Herring, H. 1961. *A History of Latin America from the Beginnings to the Present*. New York: Knopf.

Hitti, O. 1967. *History of the Arabs*. New York: St. Martins.

Hooks, J. 1947. Women's Occupation Through Seven Decades. *Women's Bureau Bulletin 218*. U.S. Department of Labor.

Houtart, F., and Pin, E. 1965. *The Church and the Latin American Revolution*. New York: Sheed and Ward.

International Labor Review. 1953. Women's Employment in Asian Countries. 68.

Iran. 1968. Iranian Statistical Centre. *National Census of Population and Housing, 1966*. Vol. 168. *Total Country*.

Issawi, C. 1947. *Egypt: An Economic and Social Analysis*. London: Oxford University Press.

Jaffe, A. 1956. Women in the Work Force. *Monthly Labor Review* 79.

_____. 1959. *People, Jobs and Economic Development*. Glencoe: Free Press.

_____, and Azumi, K. 1960. The Birth Rate and Cottage Industries in Underdeveloped Countries. *Economic Development and Cultural Change* 9.

_____, and Stewart, D. 1951. *Manpower Resources and Utilization: Principles of Working Force Analysis*. New York: Wiley.

Kirk, G. 1963. *The Middle East: From the Rise of Islam to Modern Times*. New York: Praeger.

Kiser, C. W., Grabill, W. H., and Campbell, A. 1968. *Trends and Variations in Fertility in the United States*. Cambridge: Harvard University Press.

Klein, V. 1963/1964. Industrialization and the Changing Role of Women. *Current Sociology* 12(1).

Korson, H. 1969. Student Attitude Towards Mate Selection in a Muslim Society: Pakistan. *Journal of Marriage and Family Living* 31.

Lacouture, J., and Lacouture, S. 1958. *Egypt in Transition.* New York: Criterion.

Levy, R. 1965. *The Social Structure of Islam.* Cambridge: Cambridge University Press.

Libya. 1966. Census and Statistical Department. *General Population Census of Libya 1964.* Tripoli.

Lorrimer, F. 1959. *Culture and Human Fertility.* Paris: UNESCO.

Lughod, J. A. 1965. The Emergence of Differential Fertility in Urban Egypt. *Milbank Memorial Fund Quarterly* 45(2).

McGinnis, N. 1966. Marriage and Family in Middle Class Mexico. *Journal of Marriage and Family Living* 28.

Mexico. 1962. Dirección General de Estadística. *VIII Censo General de Población 1960.* Mexico, D.F.

Miro, C. A., and Rath, F. 1965. Preliminary Findings of Comparative Fertility Surveys in Three Latin American Countries. *Milbank Memorial Fund Quarterly* 43(2), Pt. II.

Morocco. Undated. Service Central des Statisques. *Résultats du Recensement de 1960,* Vol. II. Rabat.

Myrdal, A., and Klein, V. 1956. *Women's Two Roles: Home and Work.* London: Routledge and Kegan Paul.

National Manpower Council. 1957. *Manpower.* New York: Columbia University Press.

Patai, R. 1952. The Middle East as a Culture Area. *Middle East Journal* 6(1).

_____. 1955. The Dynamics of Westernization in the Middle East. *Middle East Journal* 9(1).

Peristiany, J. G. 1965. *Honour and Shame: Values of Mediterranean Society.* London: Weidenfeld and Nicolson.

Peru. 1964. Dirección Nacional de Estadística y Censos. *Sexto Censo Nacional de Población, 1961.* Lima.

Pike, F., ed. 1964. *Conflict Between Church and State in Latin America.* New York: Knopf.

Pratt, L. V., and Whelpton, P. K. 1956. Social and Psychological Factors Affecting Fertility. *Milbank Memorial Fund Quarterly* 34.

Reguena, M. 1965. Social and Economic Correlates of Induced Abortion in Santiago, Chile. *Demography* 2.

Ridley, J. C. 1959. Number of Children Expected in Relation to Non-Familial Activities of Wife. *Milbank Memorial Fund Quarterly* 37.

Rivlin, B., and Szyliowicz, J. 1965. *The Contemporary Middle East Tradition and Innovation.* New York: Random House.

Schurz, W. 1954. *This New World: The Civilization of Latin America.* New York: Dutton.

_____. 1963. *Latin America: A Descriptive Survey.* New York: Dutton.

Simic, A. 1969. Management of the Male Image in Yugoslavia. *Anthropological Quarterly* 42.

Smith, L. 1955. Demographic Factors Related to Economic Growth in Brazil. In *Economic Growth: Brazil, India, Japan,* eds. S. Kuznets, S. Moore, and J. Spengler. Durham: Duke University Press.

Stavenhagen, R. 1970. Classes, Colonialism and Acculturation. In *Masses in Latin America,* ed. I. Horowitz. New York: Oxford University Press.

Stycos, J. M. 1965. Female Employment and Fertility in Peru. *Milbank Memorial Fund Quarterly* 43(1).

_____, and Back, K. 1964. *The Control of Human Fertility in Jamaica.* New York: Cornell University Press.

_____, and Weller, R. 1967. Female Working Roles and Fertility. *Demography* 4.

Syria. 1962. Ministry of Planning, Directorate of Statistics. *Census of Population 1960.*

Tabah, L. 1963. A Study of Fertility in Santiago, Chile. *Journal of Marriage and Family Living* 25(1).

_____. 1964. Comparative Surveys of Fertility in Latin America. *Population* 19.

135

_____, and Samuel, R. 1962. Preliminary Findings of a Survey on Fertility and Attitudes Towards Family Formation in Santiago, Chile, In *Research in Family Planning,* ed. C. V. Kiser. Princeton: Princeton University Press.

Turkey. 1969. State Institute of Statistics. *Census of Population 1965. Social and Economic Characteristics of Population.* Ankara.

United Nations, Population Division. 1953. *The Determinants and Consequences of Population Trends.* Population Studies #17, ST/SOA/Ser. A-17. New York.

_____, Department of Economic and Social Affairs. 1965. *Demographic Yearbook 1964--Population Census Statistics III.* New York.

_____, International Labor Office. 1968. *Yearbook of Labor Statistics 1967.* Geneva: United Nations Publications, 27th ed.

_____, Department of Economic and Social Affairs. 1969. *Demographic Yearbook 1968.* New York: United Nations.

_____, International Labor Office. 1970. *Yearbook of Labor Statistics 1969.* Geneva: United Nations Publications, 29th ed.

UNESCO. 1970. *UNESCO Statistical Yearbook 1969.* New York: UNESCO Publications Center.

U.S. Department of Commerce, Bureau of the Census. 1960. *United States Census of Population 1960--Occupational Characteristics.* Washington, D.C.: U.S. Government Printing Office.

_____. 1960. *Historical Statistics of the United States: Colonial Times to 1957.* Washington, D.C.: U.S. Government Printing Office.

Vallier, I. 1967. Religious Elites: Differentiations and Developments in Roman Catholicism. In *Elites in Latin America,* eds. S. Lipset and A. Solari. New York: Oxford University Press.

_____. 1970. *Catholicism, Social Control and Modernization in Latin America.* New Jersey: Prentice Hall.

Venezuela. 1967. Dirección General de Estadística y Censos Nacionales. *Novene Censo General de Población 1961. Resumen General de la República, Partes B.C.* Caracas.

136

Wagley, C. 1968. *The Latin American Tradition*. New York: Columbia University Press.

Warshaw, J. 1922. *The New Latin America*. New York: Crowell.

Wilensky, H. 1968. Women's Work: Economic Growth, Ideology and Social Structure. *Industrial Relations* 7(3).

Willems, E. 1953. Structure of the Brazilian Family. *Social Forces* 31.

Witteck, P. 1938. L'Arabisation de l'Orient Semitique. *Revue des Études Islamiques* 12.

Wolfbein, S. L., and Jaffe, A. 1964. Demographic Factors in Labor Growth. *American Sociological Review* 11(3).

Woodsmall, R. 1956. *The Study of the Role of Women in Lebanon, Egypt, Iraq, Jordan and Syria 1954-1955*. New York: International Federation of Business and Professional Women.

INDEX

ERRATA

p. viii (contents, title Chapter 6): <u>should read</u> The Role of the
Family in the Structure of Social Control

p. ix (List of Tables, title Table 7): <u>should read</u> Distribution of
the Total Non-Agricultural Labor Force by Economic Branches
of Activity: Selected Countries in Latin America and the
Middle East.
(title Table 9): <u>should read</u> Female Proportion of Total Non-
Agricultural Economically Active Population Within Specific
Occupational Categories and Industrial Activity Branch: Selected Countries in Latin America and the Middle East.

P. x (title Table 12): <u>for</u> Female Populations, <u>read</u> Female Population

p. 23 (title Table 7): <u>should read</u> as in p. ix above

p. 27 (title Table 9): <u>should read</u> as in p. ix above

p. 46 (title Table 12): <u>should read</u> as in p. x above

p. 47 (paragraph 3, line 2): <u>for</u> on average, <u>read</u> on the average

p. 82 (chapter title): <u>should read</u> as in p. viii above